AF575639

Portable Patchwork

The Women Pioneers of the Original Quick & Easy Quilting Method, with Projects for Today

Pamela Weeks

OTHER SCHIFFER BOOKS BY PAM WEEKS

Civil War Quilts, coauthor Donald Beld, ISBN 978-0-7643-5888-3

Deeds Not Words: Celebrating 100 Years of Women's Suffrage, coauthor Sandra Sider, ISBN 978-07643-5917-0

OTHER SCHIFFER BOOKS ON RELATED SUBJECTS

Quilting with Doilies: Inspiration, Techniques, and Projects, by Barbara Polston, ISBN 978-0-7643-4699-6

Quiltings, Frolics & Bees: 100 Years of Signature Quilts, by Sue Reich, ISBN 978-0-7643-4098-7

Library of Congress Control Number: 2020952775

Cover and interior design by Ashley Millhouse
Photography by Pamela Weeks, unless otherwise noted.

Type set in PT Serif/PT Sans

ISBN: 978-0-7643-6202-6
Printed in Serbia

Published by Schiffer Publishing, Ltd.
4880 Lower Valley Road
Atglen, PA 19310
Phone: (610) 593-1777; Fax: (610) 593-2002
E-mail: Info@schifferbooks.com
Web: www.schifferbooks.com

Presented to
Mrs. C.H. Vaughn
by
Sunshine Circle
Christmas 1928
Georgia
Ivy
L. WHITCOMB
1928

Contents

Joann Weeks Bailey wrote a book on the history of Northwood, New Hampshire, published in 1976. She enlisted me to draw the maps and letter some of the illustrations. When she presented me with my copy, I remember thinking that someday I would like to write a book, and I did—two so far. I dedicate my second book on quilt history to her, my second mother, my guiding star.

ACKNOWLEDGMENTS

I want to thank the many people and organizations who generously assisted me in my research and whose encouragement and contributions resulted in this book.

Stephanie Hatch, Deb and Dick Grana, Cynthia Black, and Wendy Reed were collectors and researchers long before me and gave me the support and courage to take on this project. Lori Stubbs, Diane Shink, Lynda Chenowith, Kay and Lori Triplett, Lynne Evans Miller, Mary Koval, and Julie Silber shared not only the quilts found in their travels and in their keeping but also their knowledge. Stephanie Drake found the 1877 reference to quilt as you go in *The Ladies' Guide to Needle Work, and Susan Miller sent the pattern from the 1950 Farm Journal for the Tulip Patch (potholder) quilt.* Sandra Munsey guided me through the genealogy of the Locke family, and I have continued to use the research methods I learned from her ever since. Jane Lury, Laura Fisher, and Cindy Rennels are highly respected textile dealers who tempted me on many occasions (sometimes successfully) to enlarge my personal collection.

Staff and volunteers at the following institutions and organizations were both helpful and generous: Wenham Museum, Wenham, Massachusetts; Dennis Historical Society, Dennis, Massachusetts; Manchester Historic Association, Manchester, New Hampshire; Winterthur Museum, Winterthur, Delaware; Bangor Historical Society, Bangor, Maine; Brick Store Museum, Kennebunk, Maine; Hamlin Memorial Library, Paris Hill, Maine; Maine State Museum, Augusta, Maine; Maine Historical Society, Portland, Maine; New England Quilt Museum, Lowell, Massachusetts; Museum of Our National Heritage, Lexington, Massachusetts; Historic New England, Boston, Massachusetts; Wakefield Historical Society, Wakefield, Massachusetts; International Quilt Museum, University of Nebraska–Lincoln, Lincoln, Nebraska; New Hampshire Historical Society, Concord, New Hampshire; Bradford Historical Society, Bradford, New Hampshire; Mystic Seaport Museum, Mystic, Connecticut; Smithsonian Institution, Washington, DC; Museum of the Daughters of the American Revolution, Washington, DC; Colonial Williamsburg, Williamsburg, Virginia.

Gerald Roy, after appraising my first three potholder quilts, said, "I don't know what they are, so YOU go do the work and figure this out!"

The Potholder Posse is now a large group of people who send me information about the potholder quilts they find in books, in periodicals, on the internet, and in online auctions. There are many, but I want to particularly thank Carol Born, Lisa Erlandson, Carol Gebel, and Lorie Stubbs. The donors of blocks to the quilt that was the result of my empirical research are a subset of this wonderful crowd.

Don Beld peppered me with questions about potholder quilts while he was doing his own research, and we decided to collaborate on the book *Civil War Quilts*. We discovered together how many of the surviving Civil War soldiers' quilts were made block by block, and those are featured in this book in chapter 5. Don loved Civil War history and making quilts potholder style; he made thousands of blocks for hundreds of projects. I proudly possess one that he gave to me, made from the blocks in the how-to section of *Civil War Quilts*. The quilt is featured on page 149.

Molly Mahoney stepped in and saved me from data madness, ably creating a new database and interpreting the data.

Joanna Evans is an editor sent from above.

Lorie Chase has long been a friend and mentor and was the first to tell me to get serious about this research.

Scott Kimball showed up in my life just in time to support me through this and other adventures. This work would not be possible without him.

INTRODUCTION

In 1999, the purchase of a quilt constructed of individually bound blocks led me to search for additional examples.

I hoped to discover a source for this peculiar way of making a quilt. Typically, quilt construction involves making blocks and sewing them together to create a top of the desired size. Then, this top is layered with a backing, some kind of filling—often called the batting—is placed between them, and all the layers are quilted together. The word "quilt" refers to the completed item and to the stitching that holds the three layers (top, batting, and backing) together. Quilt as you go (QAYG) quilts are made in smaller sections where the top, batting, and backing are quilted together *before* the sections are joined to make a larger quilt. There are many ways to join these sections, and one of them involves finishing each block as if it were a small, one-block quilt—just like a potholder used in the kitchen. I use the term "potholder quilt" (which can also be thought of as a portable patchwork quilt) to refer to the latter construction technique. If you took a potholder quilt apart, you would have a stack of completely finished blocks.

The earliest known potholder quilts date to the early nineteenth century. At that time, the object used to protect one's hands from hot objects was called a "kettle holder." I adopted the term "potholder" rather than kettle holder to describe the technique, because today it is rarely necessary to explain what a potholder is.

The collection of data from 151 potholder quilts and seven collections of individual blocks, and the physical examination of many of them, suggests that the technique emerged as a local variation within a larger national tradition of inscribed quilts. Many examples are signed and dated, documenting their functions as friendship, presentation, and fundraising quilts. Secondarily, quilts made in sections are useful for practicing sewing-machine skills, and many of the nineteenth-century quilts include blocks that are machine-quilted, machine-appliquéd, bound by machine, or a combination of these. (Mass production of home sewing machines began in the 1850s, and they were commercially available soon after.)

Researching this book led to the realization that a field guide to the many forms of QAYG was needed, since there are so many different ways to make a quilt in smaller sections, some with subtle variations. The first chapter shows and explains examples of the various techniques to help in identification, while the remainder of the book concentrates on some of the best examples of potholder quilts and the stories they tell. The appendixes contain four projects with instructions on two common and one novelty way to make small sections, joining them to make a larger quilt.

Genesee Valley Friendship Quilt, 2019. Made by members of the Genesee Valley Quilt Club, Rochester, New York. Cotton, silk, 91" by 91". Christine Wickert organized this gorgeous quilt for the group's annual raffle. *Private collection; photo by David Braitsch*

CHAPTER 1

A FIELD GUIDE TO QUILT AS YOU GO

Quilt as you go (QAYG) is a popular technique for creating a quilt in sections, which are quilted to hold the three layers (top, batting, and backing) together *before* the sections are stitched together to form a larger quilt.

Working in sections makes quilting easier. When quilting by hand, no large quilt-sized frame is needed. You can quilt the sections in your lap or with a small frame. If quilting by machine, small sections are easier to run through a home sewing machine. In the words of one machine-quilting teacher, there is no pushing a large quilt through a small hole (the space between the sewing-machine needle and the machine body), which reduces strain on the quilter's upper body. When working in smaller sections, you might consider using thicker batting to give more depth to the work. Working in sections makes the project portable—it can easily be carried out of the home or studio and worked on anywhere. Also, these smaller sections are easier to store while the quilt is being made.

Another benefit is that there are no long intervals of doing just one procedure, because you can choose to piece or appliqué a few blocks, then layer and quilt these, and then go back to block construction, returning later to more quilting. In QAYG there is no need for one large piece of backing fabric, and smaller pieces of batting left over from other projects can be used.

Many quilts made in the second half of the nineteenth century by using QAYG techniques are partially or completely machine-quilted. It is generally easier to use a stationary sewing machine for quilting if the sections are smaller than a bed-sized quilt. An inscribed quilt (probably made around 1860) in my collection has pieced blocks alternating with white setting blocks. The setting blocks are intricately hand-quilted with a curved paisley shape in all but one block, and it is quilted in the same pattern by machine. More than half of the potholder quilts made for Civil War soldiers exhibit machine quilting on the surface, and I recorded several presentation or fundraising quilts made in the last quarter of the nineteenth century that were quilted by machine.

QAYG works well for group projects, and this is why I think potholder quilts in particular are so often used for inscribed quilts meant for gifts or service donations. Each participant is given a block size and then asked to produce one or more finished blocks that are then sewn together to complete the quilt. The different steps can also be shared if some makers do not like to quilt; they can make blocks and give the quilting over to others who do.

After the block or section is pieced, appliquéd, or otherwise embellished, it is layered with batting and backing. Before quilting, the quilter should decide which joining method will be used. Some methods require leaving a certain amount of the edges of the blocks unquilted to make an easy join possible. In other methods, the blocks are made with the batting and backing fabric cut larger than the front, and in some, the joins are easier to make if each block is bordered with strips of fabric called sashing.

The variations for joining QAYG sections are many. The most commonly used are included here and can be grouped as follows:

Backing brought to front after seaming

Seamed finish (flat-fold seams)

Backing brought to front after seaming: Blocks are layered with batting cut ½" larger and backing cut 1½" larger. Quilt the block, then place two block backs together and stitch a seam just through the backings, narrowly missing the batting. Press the seam open and turn under the edges, covering the edge of the patchwork/appliqué block. Hand or machine stitch in place. Repeat, sewing all the blocks together in rows, then sew the rows together in the same manner. The outer blocks' backings are turned under and sewn down, forming a binding. Here again, the machine top-stitching used to secure the turned-under edges will tend to make the quilt stiff.

Seamed finish (flat-fold seams): The top sections are seamed right sides together, with batting and backing folded back to prevent them from getting caught in the seam, which is then pressed open or to the side. Next, the batting is trimmed so the edges meet and are secured with lightweight fusible webbing to hold the batting edges in place. One side of the backing is smoothed out flat, and then the other side is folded over it, the raw edge turned under, and sewn down with a blind stitch. The process can be reversed so that the backing of the blocks is sewn together, the batting is butted as described, and the top edges of the block are sewn one over the other. This technique is most often finished by hand, but if the seams are lined up properly, machine topstitching will hold the turned edge in place. There are two advantages to this method. When carefully done, it is hard to detect, and when sewn by hand, the quilt is unlikely to be stiff.

Seamed finish (strip-covered seam)

Seamed finish (strip-covered seam): All three of the quilted layers of the blocks are squared and trimmed to the same size. The blocks are sewn together through all layers, and the seams are graded, or trimmed, to reduce bulk. Strips of fabric with raw edges folded under are applied over the seams, usually on the back. The disadvantage of this method, especially if the blocks are small, is a finished quilt that is rather stiff.

Inserted component finish (piping)

Inserted component finish (piping): Several methods of joining blocks by inserting fabric elements exist. The earliest examples I found have piping inserted between the quilted blocks. Piping is made by sewing a strip of fabric over a cotton cord. A block is placed faceup, with piping laid on next with a second block laid facedown, completing the sandwich with all raw edges lined up. Stitching goes through all the layers, and then the raw edges are secondarily secured with an overcast stitch. There is an inscribed quilt, circa 1850 and made in Boston, in the collection of the International Quilt Museum, University of Nebraska–Lincoln, that is constructed of red appliqué motifs on a white background with red piping inserted between the blocks and the borders. I found on eBay two more quilts of the same era that were constructed in this way and are now in my collection.

Inserted component finish (strips inserted front and back)

Inserted component finish (strip covering on the back)

Inserted component finish (strips inserted front and back): Strips of fabric are sewn into the seams that join the sections. A doubled binding strip is placed on the top of one block, and a narrower single strip is placed on the back and sewn. Then, the next block is sewn to the narrow strip on the back of the first block, which joins them and draws the edges together so that they are butted. The doubled strip on the top of the first block is folded over to cover the butted seam and is sewn in place by machine or hand.

Inserted component finish (strip covering on the back): Quilted sections are joined with a ¼-inch seam through all the layers, including a folded binding strip in the seam on the back of the block or section. The seam allowances on the back of the blocks are either forced over to one side or pressed open, and the binding strip is sewn down to cover the seam allowances. The advantages are that the technique is simple to do, it is unnoticeable on the quilt top, and you can quilt to the edge of the section. As for disadvantages, the seam is bulky and resists lying flat, it is very noticeable on the back, and the binding should be sewn down by hand. This method is best done with a thin batting.

Butted sections

Quilted as constructed (QAC)

Butted sections: The quilted sections are squared and trimmed. Section edges are butted against each other and then whipstitched or zigzag-stitched together. Strips of fabric are applied to cover the stitching, sometimes on both the top and the back of the quilt.

Quilted as constructed (QAC):
Generally, the section is pieced and quilted at the same time by layering the backing, right side down, and laying the batting on it. The piecing—usually log cabin, strips, or crazy piecing—is applied to the batting and sewn through all layers. Some authors also call this "sew & flip," "sew & quilt," or "one-step quilting." The finished sections are then joined by one of the methods listed above—most often using flat-fold seams.

Books covering a wide range of quilt as you go techniques

Examples of yo-yo and cathedral windows

There are many variations of QAC, including one found in Val Freeman's *Guide to Quilted Appliqué* in which only appliqué patterns are given with several methods of joining blocks. In *Crazy Shortcut Quilts: Quilt as You Go and Finish in Half the Time!*, Margarita McManus and Sarah Raffuse present a crazy-quilt variation in which blocks are pieced and then quilted to the batting and backing with decorative machine embroidery stitches. The blocks are joined with a top and back, simultaneously applied sashing, which is in turn topstitched with decorative machine embroidery stitches.

Rag, or frayed-edge, quilts, are made by sewing layered raw-edge multilayer blocks of fabric together with the seams left exposed on the top of the quilt. The ½-inch seams are snipped perpendicular to the seam (but taking care not to cut the seam) to increase the amount of fraying when the completed quilt is washed and dried. Three to five layers of various fabrics that fray easily (the use of cotton flannel is common) are stacked, lightly machine-quilted, then joined. Finally, the quilt is washed and dried by machine.

QAYG novelty methods: While not true quilts because there are not three layers held together with stitching, these units are completed and then joined.

Yo-yos are made by cutting fabric circles, hemming the edges, and then using a running stitch, gathering the circles until they pucker into smaller circles and tying them off securely. This technique was popular in the 1930s and 1940s and enjoyed a brief revival in the 1970s. Cathedral window units start with large squares of fabric folded in on themselves—similar to an Origami project—and sewn together. Small bits of fabric are placed on the squares, their edges folded over and sewn down to finish the unit.

Biscuit quilts, named for the three-dimensional shape of each unit, are made by stitching together two squares of fabric of different sizes. A tuck is taken in each of the four sides of the larger piece of fabric to make the sides the same length as the sides on the smaller square. The two squares are then stitched together, leaving an opening so that stuffing can be inserted into each unit. The puffy units are then stitched together. Usually a backing is applied to the entire comforter once the "biscuit" units have been stitched together.

Detail, Biscuit cushion cover

Detail of pillow quilt

A box of partially worked pillow components

Pillow quilts (which I classify as potholder quilts) are made up of small, individually crafted pillows and are included in greater detail in chapters 6 and 8. The pillows are stuffed with batting and then finished with a knife edge, in which the edges of the pillow fabrics are turned under toward each other and sewn invisibly together. Graphic Enterprises published *Stuff ' n' Puff Quilts*, a 1976 pattern book for quilts made of small pillows. The directions given are simple: "You sew front and back (of the pattern pieces) at the same time leaving a small opening for stuffing; therefore, no lining, no interlining, no frame. They are totable, easily available to stitch at home, in the car, while waiting or whenever a spare moment arises."[1] Once the pattern pieces are sewn, they are turned to the right side, pressed, and filled with loose batting of the sort used for making stuffed toy animals. The opening is sewn closed, and the multitudes of small blocks are then whipstitched together to form the desired pattern. There is a note in the instructions suggesting that the units may be "joined on the sewing machine using a zig-zag stitch in a contrasting or harmonizing color thread."

Envelope quilts are potholder quilts constructed by placing a square of fabric right side down. On it is centered a piece of batting ½ inch smaller, so that ¼ inch of the fabric square is seen on each side of the square of batting. The sides of the fabric square are pressed up and over the batting, enclosing all edges. It is then folded in half on the diagonal to form an isosceles triangle, and those edges are sewn together to close the pillow unit. The individual pillows, or envelopes, are then sewn together. When colors are carefully chosen and arranged, many traditional patchwork patterns can be achieved with the triangles.

POTHOLDER CONSTRUCTION TECHNIQUES AND VARIATIONS

With other quilt as you go methods, each unit is pieced, appliquéd, or left as one piece of fabric, then layered and quilted individually. The raw edges are left unfinished until the quilted blocks, or sections made of multiple quilted blocks, are joined together, typically by seaming the patterned top, right sides together, then either turning under the seams on the backside, applying a strip of fabric over the seam, or simply leaving the seam exposed. Many nineteenth-century log cabin quilts are constructed this way.

In contrast, not only are the blocks of potholder quilts layered and quilted individually, but the edges are finished before the blocks are joined. Regarding construction, each potholder block could stand alone as a finished one-block quilt. The finished blocks are usually whipstitched together from the back—not seamed—to form a larger quilt. Some quilts have blocks joined with a hidden ladder stitch, and three were found sewn together by machine.

The predominant method for finishing potholder quilt blocks is to apply binding. In most nineteenth-century quilts, straight-grain binding is applied around the block, starting and finishing on one corner. Several quilts from this time period have blocks that were finished by applying the binding to opposite sides of the blocks, and some are very haphazard, seeming to use up strips that might cover one, two, or three sides of a block, then applying smaller pieces of binding as needed.

Most block makers took care while applying binding to turn the corners carefully, making tight and square turns, but others seemed more casual about their corners, nearly rounding them. The tight corners leave no gaps when the blocks are sewn together, whereas the rounded corners leave small openings where four blocks come together. I documented three quilts that covered these openings with embroidery, crocheted rosettes, or pom-poms made of thin cotton string, which added an interesting decorative element to the quilt surface.

Detail of the Fisherville Friendship Quilt (page 69), showing perfectly turned corners on each block

Detail of the Crosses and Losses Quilt (page 131), showing rounded block corners

Detail of a single block with the knife-edge finish. Notice the basting stitches left in place.

Detail of the Captain Wilson Quilt (page 66), showing the intersection of four knife-edge finished blocks. *Courtesy of the Cumberland Historical Society, Cumberland, Maine*

Detail of the back of a quilt, showing the intersection of four blocks with the knife-edge finish

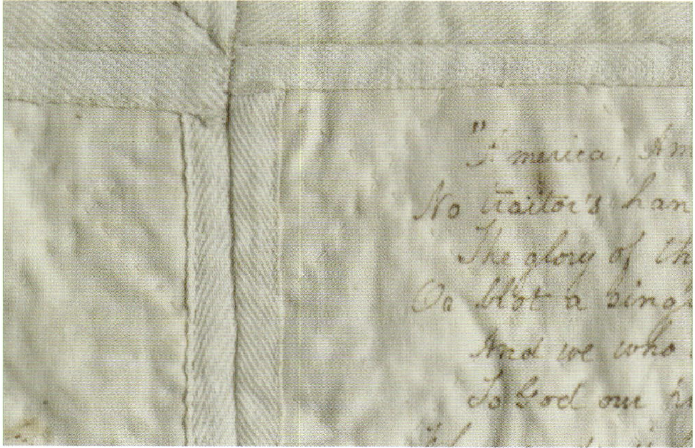

Detail of the Portland Album Quilt (page 90), showing blocks finished with woven tape. *Courtesy of the Maine State Museum, Augusta, Maine, 2015.11.1*

In the second-most-commonly-found method of finishing the edges of the blocks, the edges of both the top and the back fabrics are turned in on themselves, basted together, and sewn invisibly (with a whipstitch or ladder stitch). This is termed a "knife-edge" finish. Early on, I examined a set of individual blocks with knife-edge finishing at the Wenham Museum in Massachusetts and saw for the first time the basting stitches that held the edges together. The edges of one of the blocks in the set had been invisibly sewn together, using a stitch similar to the ladder stitch. When assembled into a quilt, blocks with the knife-edge finish appear to make up a traditional quilt constructed with blocks sewn together *before* layering and quilting, because there is no individual block binding evident. From the back, it is easier to see that the blocks are finished and have been whipstitched together.

I have a suspicion that not all blocks with a knife-edge finish in a potholder quilt had their edges sewn before being sewn together in the quilt. It would not be necessary to sew the edge twice, if both edges of each block were sewn to both edges of the next block in their joining.

Several potholder quilts from the nineteenth century have blocks that are finished with woven tape; the blocks of one silk quilt are finished with black silk ribbon. The tape or ribbon is simply folded in half and sewn over the raw edges of the block. When working on a reproduction of a Civil War soldier's quilt, I was able to attach the woven tape binding by taking small stitches from the front of the block and through the tape on the back—a quick and easy way to bind the blocks.

Detail of the reverse of the Emily Munroe Pictorial Quilt (page 33). *Courtesy of the New England Quilt Museum, Lowell, Massachusetts, 2000.2; Photo by David Stansbury*

Another way to finish individual blocks is to turn the top or front fabric to the back of the block (or the backing fabric to the front of the block) and turn the edges under. Both the New England Quilt Museum and Historic New England hold appliquéd and embroidered mid-nineteenth-century wool quilts made block by block. To construct each finished block, the front fabric was cut an inch (or more) larger all around than the backing fabric. The two fabrics were layered together, and the appliqué and embroidery stitches were done through both layers; there is no batting in these two quilts. Then, the front fabric was folded over and coarsely whipped to the backing fabric, and the blocks were then whipstitched together.

In the 1970s, Graphic Enterprises published a series of softcover books on quilting, including several on various methods of quilt as you go. Two of them, *Envelope Patchwork* in 1978 and *Add a Block Quilts* in 1979, provide instructions for blocks made by cutting the lining, or backing, of the block into interesting repeating shapes, folding in the raw edges, turning it up, and stitching it over the batting and material composing the top or front of the block. When folded to the front of the block, the repeating shapes produced hearts, stars, butterflies, and other complex patterns. Only one example was found using this technique, and it was one of the least complicated patterns—a hexagon with rounded edges.

Two quilts with English provenance were documented in my original study of potholder quilts. Backings were cut for each block, and then the edges were turned to the front, with the corners carefully folded. Printed fabric shapes with turned-under edges were then appliquéd on top of the turned edges, creating finished blocks.

Several contemporary quilters are making individually finished blocks by cutting the backing for each block larger than the front. The block is pieced or appliquéd and then quilted, and then the backing is turned to the front and turned under, leaving a finished, bound edge.

Detail of the Gebel English Quilt, showing the folded-up and under-edge finish

Detail of block construction in progress, with the backing turned up and over the front of the block, and the top fabric edges turned under and stitched down over backing fabric.

CHAPTER 2

THE SEARCH FOR THE ORIGIN OF POTHOLDER QUILTS

I fell in love with inscribed quilts many years ago and began collecting and researching them, always searching for any that might contain my family names.

Detail of the embroidered top border of the Sarah A. Leavitt Quilt, dated December 16, 1847 (see full quilt on page 48)

I am of the tenth generation in my family to live in New Hampshire, and I reasoned that if I searched long and hard, I would find a quilt with the name of one of my antecedents. An auction house advertised a quilt with one of the family names, and, because I was going to be in Europe at the time, I asked my aunt Joann Weeks Bailey to purchase the quilt for me. When I returned, I called Aunt Jo to see if she had obtained the quilt. She asked me to come look at it, because she described it as the weirdest thing she had ever seen. When I examined my new quilt, I found the name and date "Sarah A. Leavitt, December 16, 1847" embroidered in cross-stitch across a border attached to the top of the quilt and decorated with dark-blue crocheted lace.

Detail of the Sarah A. Leavitt Quilt. *Photo by David Bohl*

The quilt is composed of LeMoyne star blocks set on point. The stars were pieced from dark-blue silk damask against red cotton, alternating with whole blocks of pale-yellow silk. Each star block was individually bound with dark-blue silk, the yellow blocks were bound with pale-blue silk, and the blocks were closely whipstitched together on the back. It seemed that the maker had finished each block like an elegant 11-inch-square potholder and then joined them to make a quilt. I was mystified by the elaborate block-by-block construction technique. I needed some way to reference the technique, and the term "potholder quilt" seemed a handy descriptor.

Soon after I bought the Sarah A. Leavitt quilt, I took it to the Vermont Quilt Festival, a large regional show with national-level teachers, and showed it to several certified quilt appraisers and quilt historians. They had examined quilts made with other quilt as you go techniques, but none of them had seen this particular method of construction. Four other quilt researchers and collectors whom I met around this time were familiar with the technique. Deb Grana of Albany, New York, and Stephanie Hatch of Boxford, Massachusetts, collect potholder quilts. Cyndi Black of Litchfield, Maine, and Wendy Reed of Bath, Maine, coordinated the Maine Quilt Heritage Project, which documented

French Presentation Quilt, made by the Young Ladies of the Society for Mrs. French, 1855, Hudson, New Hampshire. Cotton, 87" by 87". *Collection of the author; photo by David Bohl*

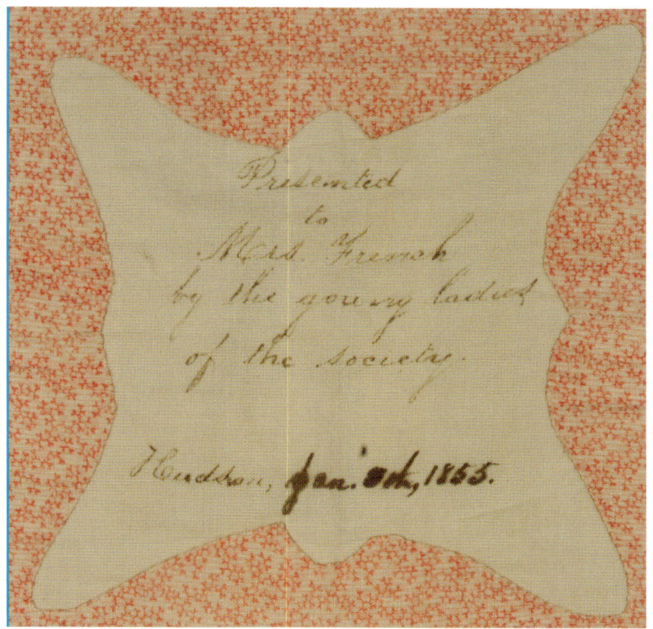

Detail of the French Presentation Quilt. *Photo by David Bohl*

nearly 3,000 quilts since 1987. Wendy Reed has made many award-winning quilts by using the technique. These women shared their collections and knowledge and encouraged me to undertake this research.

I began my search for the origin of potholder quilts by searching published sources, looking through hundreds of instruction manuals, state documentation project books, published museum collections, exhibition catalogs, and other online materials. Between October 2006 and July 2019, I contacted curators of national and regional museums with large quilt collections, including the DAR Museum, the Smithsonian Institution, the International Quilt Museum, the New England Quilt Museum, Colonial Williamsburg, and the Virginia Quilt Museum. I visited or contacted the major historical museums in New England, as well as a number of local museums in Maine, Massachusetts, Connecticut, and New Hampshire.

In early 2003, I posted requests for information on internet LISTSERVs that yielded several contacts who had seen potholder quilts listed on eBay, in collections at museums where they volunteer, or in other small local historical associations. Others sent links to websites and additional references in books; several other virtual collections began to appear in Pinterest pages devoted to potholder quilts. Appraisers have put me in touch with their clients who own examples. I interviewed volunteers of state quilt documentation projects, including Vermont, Rhode Island, and Connecticut. I was given access to the records of the Maine and Massachusetts Quilt Documentation projects. Information from the New Hampshire Quilt Documentation Project was not available for this project.

I interviewed several dealers of antique quilts, including those who vend at the International Quilt Festival, the American Quilter's Society Show, and the American Quilt Study Group annual seminar. Laura Fisher was particularly helpful and shared four quilts from her collection. Among the private collectors I contacted, Stephanie Hatch was generous with sharing her expertise as well as her collection. At the Maine Quilt Festival in August 2006, Stephanie Hatch, Wendy Reed, and Cynthia Black curated a show of potholder quilts where I was able to document fourteen quilts and meet more collectors.

In addition to examples of potholder quilts and other quilt as you go quilts, I searched the literature for descriptions of the techniques. The January 1835 issue of *Godey's Lady's Book* suggests that making "kettle holders" of quilted patchwork and binding them with tape is a good exercise for children learning to sew, but there is no suggestion that one should make many of these and sew them together to make a quilt.[2]

The author collected several sets of finished blocks, either never joined to make a quilt or taken from a quilt, as evidenced by thread remains.

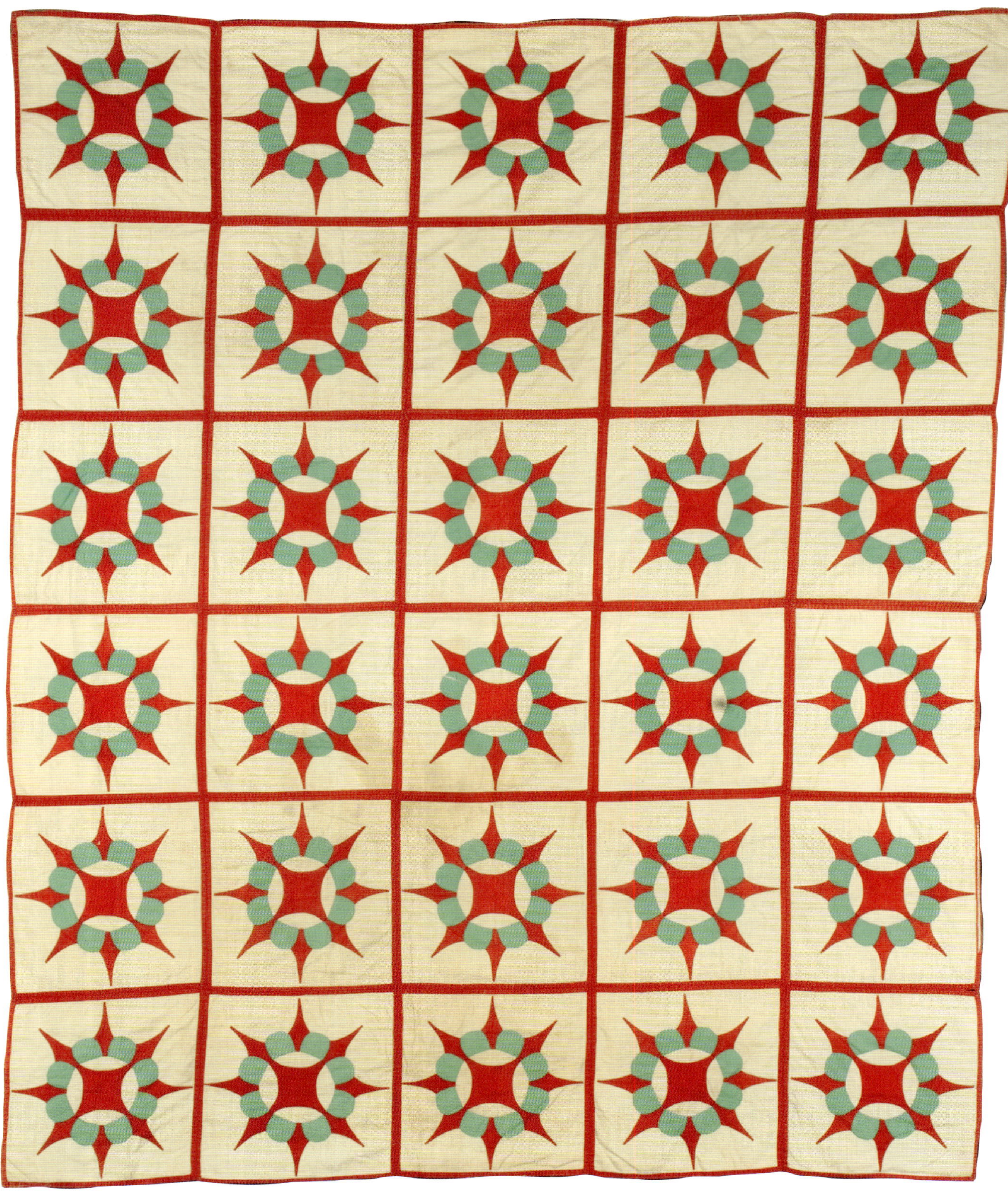

King's Crown, unknown maker, ca. 1900. Probably New England. Cotton, 89" by 89".
Collection of the author; photo by David Bohl

A Model Quilt.

I wish to tell the lady readers of the WESTERN RURAL about a "model quilt," which I helped to make. A poor family in our neighborhood, were about to move away, when a kind lady, Mrs. B., thought what a valuable gift a good quilt would be to them; so she took strips of paper and cut them in equal lengths—about 14 inches long—and sent them around to the neighboring ladies, with the request that they would piece a square of dark patchwork of any pattern, and quilt and bind it; then, when the squares were joined with a cast over stitch, the quilt was finished, and was very thankfully received.

MRS. J. C. C.

This "clipping" found by Louise Tiemann describes the making of a block-by-block quilt. "A Model Quilt" was published in the *Western Rural* 8, no. 38 (September 22, 1870): 6.

Detail of a quilt made in 1916 of actual potholders. *Photo by Dianne Shink*

In the 1877 edition of *The Ladies' Guide to Needle Work*, S. Annie Frost states:

> It is a great improvement upon the huge and unwieldy quilting-frames of the days of our grandmothers, to make the patchwork for a quilt in bound squares. Each one is lined, first with wadding, then with calico quilted neatly, and bound with strips of calico. These squares being then sewed together, the quilt is complete. Album quilts made in this way, with the name of the giver neatly written upon a small square of white in the centre of each piece, are much more acceptable than when they must all be quilted together in a huge frame.[3]

Diane Shink alerted me to a little quilt in a museum in Maplewood, Nova Scotia, Canada, and it was the first quilt I found that is actually described as a potholder quilt. One of the blocks has a loop for hanging, like those found on true potholders. An unsigned, undated exhibition label states: "The quilt is made of 55 potholders in a variety of patterns and colors, that are sewn together to make a quilt. . . . It was made in approximately 1918."[4] A second quilt made of advertising potholders appears in chapter 7.

I found many books that referred to other quilt as you go methods. Ruby McKim in 1931 described "apartment" or "compartment" quilting that "originated for the woman who lives in tiny rooms, efficiency all over. . . . The quilted sections are joined by sewing top parts with a running stitch on the wrong side. Then smooth the interlinings of cotton to overlap about one-quarter inch and sew back sections together with a blind stitch."[5]

In a 1971 book, *The Complete Guide to Machine Quilting*, Robbie and Tony Fanning describe three quilt as you go methods. They make the distinction among QAYG, that is, "making several quilt units smaller than the whole quilt and quilting each one before joining them together"; "finish-as-you-go," described as "making quilted 'pillows' with finished edges which, when joined, make a whole quilt"; and "one-step-piece-and-quilt," in which the blocks are pieced as they are sewn to the batting and backing. Further, they state that "finish-as-you-go," accomplished by making and quilting thin pillows with finished edges, is not a new idea, "having been around since the Civil War."[6] Many other authors included sections on QAYG in their books (most notably Georgia Bonesteel, whose influence will be discussed in chapter 8), but only two authors mention finishing each block before sewing the units together.

INSCRIBED QUILTS

The majority of nineteenth-century quilts made with some form of quilt as you go are inscribed. I prefer to use the term "inscribed quilt" instead of friendship, album, or signature quilt because "inscribed" is inclusive of all the possible reasons why multiple names were written on quilts in the nineteenth century.[7]

Friendship quilts are sometimes organized by a group of friends who agree to make a number of blocks to share, so that each participant receives blocks from everyone in the group. Or an individual might ask for quilt blocks of a specific size, color, or pattern. Whether the quilts resulting from these blocks are then completed individually or with the help of the group, each becomes a document of the circle of friends.

Inscribed quilts might represent the work of a group for a particular purpose. In some cases, the blocks are signed by the individuals who made them; in others, individuals make blocks that are then signed by others, or all blocks are signed by the person with the best handwriting. Inscribed quilts may be presentation quilts, created as a gift for a particular recipient. Within the private sphere of friends or family, quilts were made for a bride or for a leave-taking. In the public sphere, they were made as a token of love and respect by church congregations to honor ministers, or by students and their parents in gratitude to teachers.[8] Each of these quilts contains an inscription indicating the recipient and the purpose for the gift, and in general, the quilts in this group are the most elaborate and elegant of those in my study. These quilts have the largest blocks (measuring 16 to 22 inches square), the most-complicated piecing and appliqué, the most heavily embroidered blocks, and the most-expressive verses. This group also includes two of the three potholder quilts finished with a fringe.

Another group of inscribed quilts includes those that functioned as fundraisers for various groups and causes. Typically, the sponsoring group collects donations from individuals whose names are then inscribed on the quilt.[9] The resulting quilt is often auctioned or raffled to raise additional funds, and then it may be presented to a significant individual, taking on a secondary presentation function.

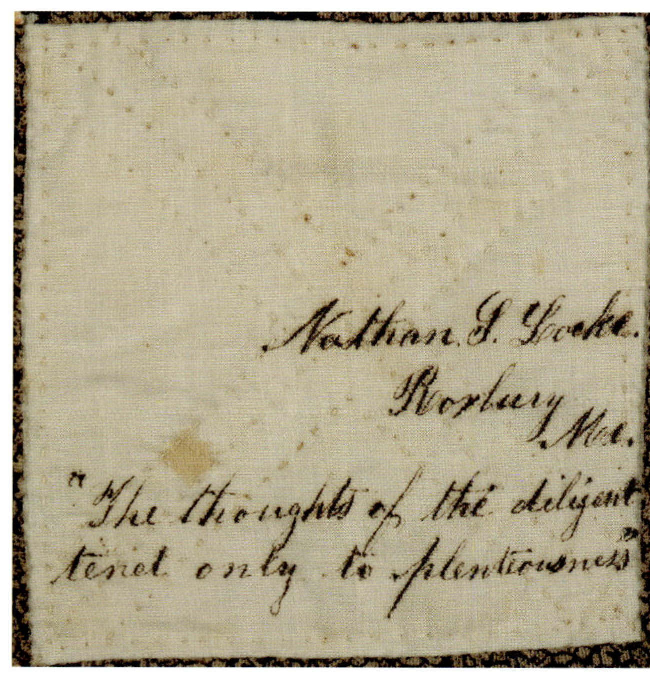

Inked inscription

Stenciled inscription

Analyzing Potholder Quilts in This Study

As of August 2019, I had identified 151 potholder quilts and seven sets of individually finished and related (but not yet sewn together) blocks. I examined many of these myself, and for others, I relied on available information from owners, curators, or published sources. Although several contemporary quilters employ the technique, I chose to focus my research on potholder quilts made before 1975. I constructed a database for systematic collection of data, including overall quilt size, block size, materials, construction techniques, intended function, and provenance. Since eighty-five of the 151 examples (56%) contain inscriptions, I constructed a separate data sheet for the signature quilts, collecting signer's names, geographical locations, and genealogical information. The earliest quilt in my sample is dated 1837; the latest, circa 1975.

Of the 120 quilts for which the geographic provenance is known, 82% are attributed to New England, and the majority of these to Maine and Massachusetts. Of this subset, 49% are attributed to Maine. This is no surprise to Stephanie Hatch, who localizes the technique to coastal Maine, centered in the area surrounding Wiscasset.[10] Folk art collector Robert Bishop, who was raised in this area of Maine, wrote in 1982: "In Friendship Album quilts from Maine, individual blocks were usually pieced or appliquéd, stuffed, and then quilted before all the blocks were sewn into a full-size quilt."[11] Massachusetts quilts compose 33% of this subset, and 12% are attributed to New Hampshire. My sample also includes three quilts made in Virginia, two made in Michigan, and one quilt each made in Indiana, Ohio, and Minnesota. Three of the quilts were made in Great Britain, and one in Nova Scotia, Canada. Several inscribed quilts attributed to places other than New England include personal names with place names from Maine, Massachusetts, or New Hampshire. The quilt attributed to Minnesota was made by women who had migrated there from Maine.[12]

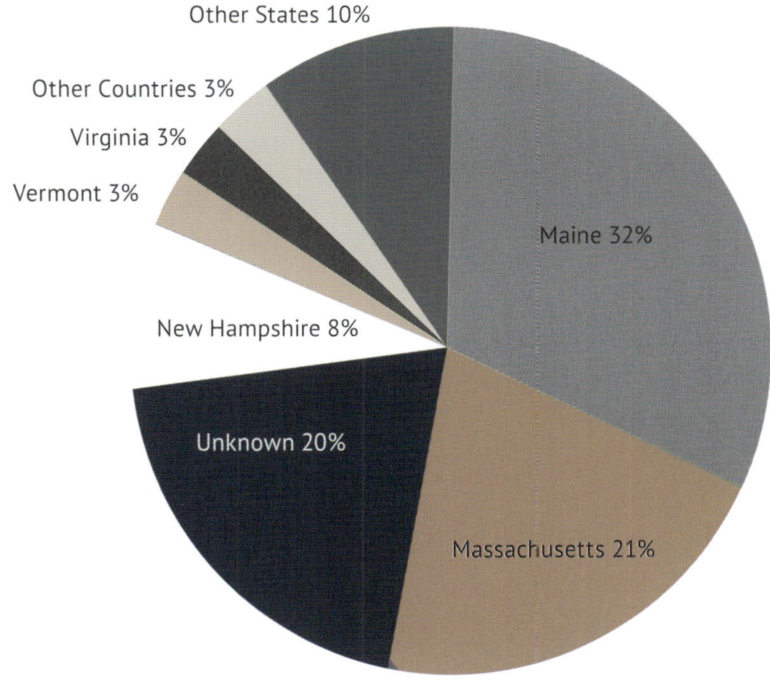

Geographic Origin of Potholder Quilts

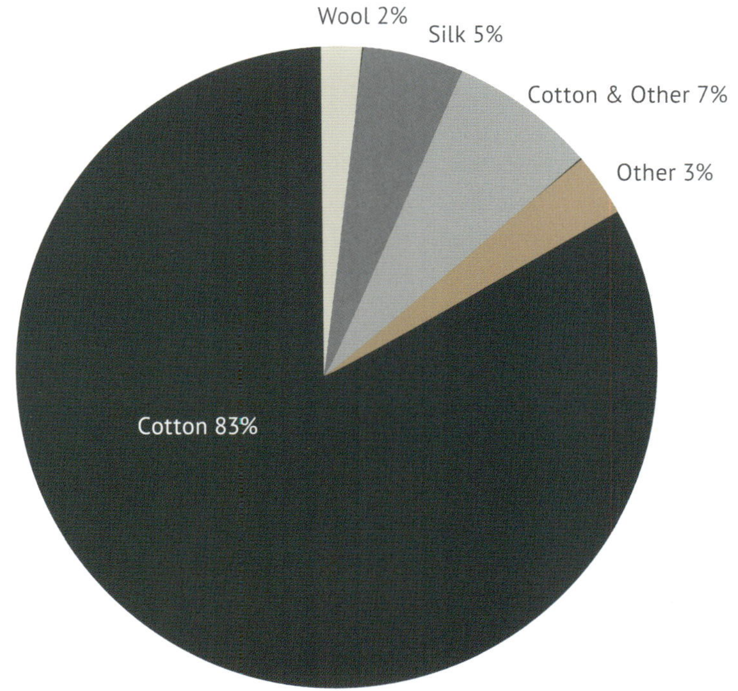

Materials Found in Potholder Blocks

Eighty-three percent of the potholder quilts are made with only cotton materials, 5% of the quilts have blocks that are all silk, and just three quilts are wool. In ten quilts, the majority of the blocks are constructed of cotton fabrics, but they include some blocks of wool or silk. Some of these quilts contain blocks that are constructed of cotton fabric and are embellished with wool, silk, or both wool and silk appliqué or embroidery.

By nature of the technique, all the quilts in the sample reflect block-style construction. Thirty-six percent of the sample contain pieced blocks. Thirty-eight percent of the sample are samplers, or "variety" quilts, to use Persis Sibley Andrews's term, containing blocks of more than one pattern.

The majority of the quilts in the sample correspond in size to typical bed quilts of the period, roughly 80 inches or more, on at least one side. The largest, a Virginia quilt dated to 1857, measures 105 by 105 inches, and the smallest, a four-block doll quilt, measures 13 inches square. The number of blocks in a quilt ranges from this four-block doll quilt to a quilt containing more than 1,000 individually bound 2-inch blocks combined with larger bound blocks pieced with eight-pointed stars. The latter quilt has the smallest block, and, at the other extreme, the quilt with the largest blocks contains twenty-three cutwork appliqué blocks measuring 22 inches square. The majority of the quilts are made of blocks that measure between 10 and 12 inches square.

Detail of a heavily quilted block from the West Falmouth, Maine, quilt

There are seven collections of related and finished but unconnected blocks. In eighty of the quilts, the blocks are set "straight," with the block edges parallel to the edge of the quilt. Twenty-nine of the quilts (20%) are set diagonally, or "on point," requiring the insertion of half-square triangles or other shapes to square up the quilt. In three of the signature quilts set on point, finished and signed blocks were cut in half, through the signatures, to make the setting triangles.

On the basis of the quilts I have examined personally, potholder blocks typically contain very thin or no batting. Clearly, these pieces were not created to function as warm bedcovers. Nearly all are quilted; the individual blocks were stabilized with stitches through all the layers. Of these, 66% are hand-quilted, 14% are machine-quilted, and 8% include both hand-quilted and machine-quilted blocks. Of the thirty quilts that evidence machine quilting, five are inscribed with dates in the 1860s, and three others, although not inscribed, appear to be from the same decade. Sixteen other quilts with machine quilting predate 1900, and the rest were made in the twentieth century.

The amount of quilting varies among the quilts; generally, the quilting is very light compared with traditionally made quilts. The stability resulting from the construction of the relatively small, individually finished units makes heavy quilting unnecessary. Within particular quilts, the quilting designs and the amount of quilting vary among the blocks. Many are quilted to pattern, following the lines of the patchwork or appliqué, and generally the quilting is seldom an important decorative element.

There are always exceptions. The blocks that are more heavily quilted are masterworks of the art. A quilt in my collection made of off-white and very fine cotton sateen has forty 10-inch blocks that are very finely quilted with a multitude of geometric and floral motifs. More than half the blocks are inscribed on the reverse, but others are not signed, and still others have small blue slips of paper containing the names that were meant to be written on a block.

The key characteristic of potholder quilts is the distinctive edge treatment of the individual blocks. In 71% of the quilts and sets of blocks, the raw edges of the three constructed layers are finished by applying a binding. Most of these are bound with folded strips of fabric, and three are bound with woven tape. Of the examples I examined personally, most of the bindings were of cotton fabric, cut with the grain, except for two bound with cotton fabric cut on the bias and three bound with silk cut with the grain. Typically, the binding was applied first to the front of

Potholder block with knife-edge finish. *Collection of the author*

Detail of an English quilt in the collection of Carol Gebel

Detail of the Emily Munroe Pictorial Quilt. *Photo by David Stansbury*

the block, then turned to the back and attached using a blind stitch. In most cases, the binding consists of a single strip, attached first to one corner of the block, continuing around the other corners, and finally ending where it began. In a few quilts, however, the binding was applied to some of the blocks in separate strips: two opposite sides of the blocks first, and then the two remaining opposite sides.

Twenty percent of the finished quilts or block sets have blocks that are finished knife edge, in which the edges of the two fabric layers are turned under, with the raw edges tucked inside the layers, and held with a running stitch or an invisible ladder stitch. Most of the variety quilts, which, by definition, consist of different-patterned blocks, also demonstrate a corresponding variety of edge finishes. Some blocks are bound with tape or fabric strips, and others have a knife-edge finish.

In two of the three examples with British provenance, the blocks are finished but have neither binding nor a knife-edge finish. The edges of the heavy off-white cotton backing fabric were folded to the front, forming a hem. Patches of printed cotton in various shapes and sizes were appliquéd to the top surface of the block like those in "tile quilts." The edges of this decorated block were turned under to form a hem around the block, creating a slightly smaller block than the backing block. This top block was then placed on the backing block, with wrong sides together, and then the top and backing blocks were slip-stitched together, with some of the backing block showing on the top as a frame around the block. These completed blocks were then stitched together to form the quilt. See quilt on page 115.

Two appliquéd and embroidered Massachusetts quilts, one dated 1854 and the other circa 1860, were constructed by lining the backs of each wool block with heavy cotton squares measuring an inch smaller than the wool block. The wool embroidery on the top surface of the block

Emily Munroe Pictorial Quilt, attributed to Emily Wiley Munroe, 1861–1865, Lynnfield, Massachusetts. Wool and cotton, 69" by 68½". *Courtesy of the New England Quilt Museum, Lowell, Massachusetts, 2000.2; photo by David Stansbury*

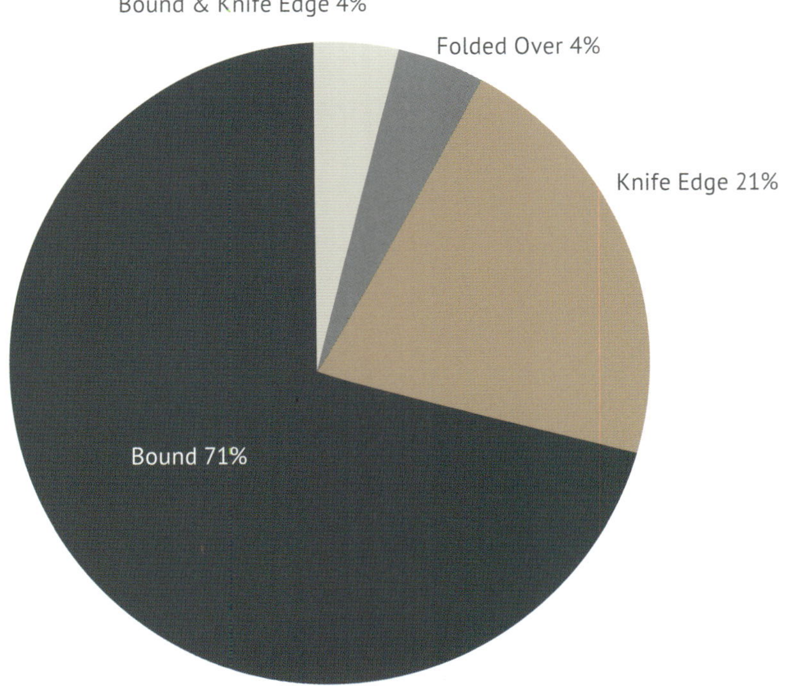

Edge Finishes of Potholder Blocks in Study

penetrates both layers, thus holding the backing in place. The blocks were finished by folding the woolen edges to the back over the cotton backing and then overcasting the wool edges in place with large stitches.[13]

In my research set, red emerged as the predominant color for binding the blocks of potholder quilts. Twenty-six percent of the 116 quilts with bound blocks are finished in red. Twenty percent of the quilts contain blocks bound in off-white, 17% in pink, and the rest in blue, green, or black. In fifteen quilts the blocks are bound in multiple colors, and in three quilts the blocks are bound with off-white woven tape.

In all but one of the sample quilts, the finished blocks were whipstitched (oversewn or overcast) together with fine, close stitches to make the full quilt. One exception is the Howard Sunday School quilt, in which the blocks were finished in a thin knife edge, and the majority of the blocks were then joined, right sides together, with a running stitch.[14] Four quilts have blocks connected with an embroidery stitch similar to the herringbone stitch, two have blocks joined by crochet, and three are joined by machine. Two of these have zigzag stitching visible on the front of the quilt.

Detail of a crazy quilt featuring red binding

EMPIRICAL RESEARCH

To better understand how potholder quilts are constructed, I made a few blocks of various sizes and edge finishes. I made a nine-block potholder crazy quilt and learned two things. First, applying binding one side at a time gave me color choices that applying a continuous binding did not (unless you piece it), and the whipstitching must be tight and even or the blocks would sag. I also found that when working by myself, it was easier to quilt and bind several blocks in the potholder method than to sew them together, layer, and quilt them in the common quilt construction method.

Next, I decided to conduct an experiment. In October 2008, I posted messages on the Quilt History List and the American Quilt Study Group LISTSERVs and asked for blocks for a potholder friendship quilt. I requested that the completed blocks be 9 inches square, be finished with a binding or knife edge, be signed with each maker's name and place of residence, have three layers (top, backing, and filling), and be accurate reproductions of mid-nineteenth-century block patterns and fabrics.

By February 2009, I had received forty-three blocks and made twenty myself. I collected the blocks in a pile on a small table near my desk and took the pile into my lap each time another arrived. I leafed through the stack as if it were an autograph book, each page signed by a friend. Unlike a collection of unfinished blocks, I did not have to worry that handling the blocks would distort them.

As expected, the blocks varied in color and pattern, but I was surprised by the complexity and detail of many of the appliqué or pieced blocks. Most participants sent a single thoughtfully designed block, and several people donated two blocks. Aunt Joann Bailey made six blocks, and she commented that it was fun to make them and gratifying to know that they were going into a larger quilt. I found that the blocks finished by the machine application of a doubled strip of fabric (a common binding method for finishing quilts today) were very stiff, while those finished with a knife edge or with hand-applied cloth binding or tape were more pliable.

Detail of Crazy Quilt. *Photo by David Bohl*

Crazy Quilt, Pamela Weeks, 2008, Durham, New Hampshire. Silk, satin, velvet, nylon ribbons, 34" by 34". The quilt was inspired by a stack of award ribbons dating to the 1960s for 4-H participation in sewing and horsemanship. The ribbons from the 1970s were won for whitewater canoe races, and those from 1993 were for winning entries in quilt shows. *Collection of the author; photo by David Bohl*

The other unexpected result was that most of the blocks conformed to the specified size. From my experience with conventional group quilts, I had expected more variation. Only three of the blocks were off by more than ¼ inch, and one by more than 1 inch. I reworked the binding of the three slightly off blocks but found I had to cut down the largest block before rebinding for it to result in the correct size.

I finished my friendship quilt quite easily. I did not have to go through joining and pressing the blocks to make the top layer of the quilt and did not have to piece and press a backing. I did not have to find a large area in which to spread out and baste together the large layers of top, batting, and backing before quilting. The process of joining the blocks was pleasurable, but occasionally tedious, and easy to pick up or put down quickly. As the quilt grew in size, I chose to assemble it in four sections to make it more manageable, rather than adding to it row by row. The time needed to finish the quilt could be measured in hours instead of days or weeks.

Because I chose to set the blocks on point rather than straight, I had the added difficulty of cutting blocks on the diagonal and binding the very sharp points thus created. I noticed full-perimeter bindings on several of the nineteenth-century quilts set on point, and realized it was an easier solution to binding half blocks individually. After setting individually bound triangular blocks across the top of the quilt, I set the half blocks on the sides of the quilt and applied a single binding to the outer edges of the quilt.

There are two disadvantages to the potholder technique. The first is the physical feel of the finished quilt. Because of the nature of the individually finished blocks, particularly those that are smaller and bound with machine-applied doubled fabric strips, and the close whipstitching required to hold them together securely, the quilt can feel stiff and does not drape well on the bed. If care is not taken in the assembly process, the joined blocks will bulge and become small hills, and the quilt will not lie flat. Washing might help, but there is the danger of losing the inscriptions in the process. I eventually realized that a single-layer binding is a better way to finish the blocks. I have made three this way, and the quilts have a softer hand.[15]

A stack of potholder blocks donated by members of the Potholder Posse

The second disadvantage is the loss of camaraderie that happens in the finishing. Assembling the blocks alone is nowhere near as much fun as sitting around a quilting frame and enjoying the quilting group or "bee." I realized that I assumed that potholder quilts were generally finished by one person, but several people could come together to join the blocks, thus preserving some of the community experience.

However, the advantages of this technique outweigh the disadvantages. If this quilt had been intended for presentation to a friend or community leader or for a fundraising project, it would have been relatively easy to conceive, organize, communicate, and complete. If the need arose to produce such a quilt in a hurry, and if enough volunteers were available to each make a block or two, a group could conceivably complete a large quilt in less than a week.

The empirical research confirmed my assertion that organizing a group project using a quilt as you go technique made the job as "finisher" relatively fast and easy and produced a quilt in short time. Blocks were contributed by a diverse group, and they were generally very high quality, showing detailed workmanship and consistent size. Several people machine-quilted their blocks—another reason to make a large quilt in small sections.

Potholder Posse Album Quilt, multiple block contributors, assembled by Pamela Weeks, 2009, Durham, New Hampshire. Cotton, 78" by 64". The author used the online LISTSERVs of the Quilt History List and the American Quilt Study Group in 2008 to request that members construct and contribute potholder blocks for a quilt. *Collection of the author*

CHAPTER 3

THE EARLIEST POTHOLDER QUILTS 1837–1850

MARGARET WYER LOCKE QUILT, 1838

Margaret Wyer Locke Quilt, 1838. Made by friends and family of the recipient, Charlestown, Massachusetts. Cotton, 71" by 50". This is the earliest known quilt constructed block by block, with inscriptions dated 1837. It was probably made for the marriage of Margaret Wyer Locke to Nathaniel Hyde. *Courtesy of the Concord Museum, Concord, Massachusetts, CM1822; photo by David Bohl*

The earliest documented block-by-block quilt construction came from Charlestown, Massachusetts, inscribed with the dates December 13, 1837, to April 1838. The quilt was likely made to celebrate the marriage of Margaret Wyer Locke to Nathaniel Hyde in September 1837, because the blocks contributed by Margaret's family and friends contain references to their relationship to Margaret, quotations, and joyful wishes indicating a journey or leave-taking.[16] The couple moved from Charlestown to New Orleans, Louisiana, where he was a hardware dealer.

Margaret Wyer Locke Hyde was born on March 30, 1807, and died on September 2, 1838, less than three weeks after the birth of her son, Thomas Locke Hyde. Nathaniel Hyde died in 1839 or 1840, and Thomas was sent to Massachusetts to live with his grandparents; the 1850 federal census lists him in their household.

This variety signature quilt combines potholder and other quilt as you go techniques. A center medallion is composed of four 11½-inch pieced or appliquéd square blocks bounded by a 2-inch-wide border of dark-brown, printed cotton. There are sixteen 8½-inch pieced square blocks arranged in a single line around a center medallion. Above and below this central area is a 3½-inch border of bias-cut dark-brown print cotton, followed by a row of four 8½-inch-square pieced blocks centered, with a half block of pink cotton at the beginning and end of each row. The sides and bottom edge of the quilt have an additional 3½-inch band of the brown border fabric. The entire perimeter is bound with a bias-cut, single layer of brown print cotton.

Most of the blocks are finished knife edge and then whipstitched together. Some blocks are joined by seaming their tops together, then folding the backing to lap one side over the other and being sewn in place, a common quilt as you go technique. The brown borders were also added in a quilt as you go fashion that is not immediately apparent.

Some of the fabrics are English chintz, with oriental and pheasant applied cutwork motifs. Other fabrics are dress prints typical of the first and early second quarter of the nineteenth century. The blocks are backed with a more crudely woven off-white cotton or linen, and one backing has printing on it and was probably a textile bag (such as a salt or grain sack) of some kind.

Detail of the center back of the Margaret Wyer Locke Quilt, showing both flat-fold seam and potholder block finishes. *Photo by David Bohl*

Margaret Wyer Locke Quilt, reverse. *Courtesy of the Concord Museum, Concord, Massachusetts, CM1822; photo by David Bohl*

Inscription from the reverse of the Margaret Wyer Locke Quilt. *Photo by David Bohl*

Detail of a block from the Margaret Wyer Locke Quilt. *Photo by David Bohl*

Twenty-five separate inscriptions appear on the backs of the blocks, and the penmanship varies with each one, indicating individual signers—a true signature quilt. The majority of the inscriptions speak of friendship with Margaret. Some wish her joy and happiness, and others ask simply to be remembered. "Dear Margaret, I often think of the pleasant hours that you have passed with me[,] and hope that you are now as happy as happy can be. Boston 1838[,] Sarah Locke." One long and lecture-filled inscription omits the writer's name but asks that Margaret guess it. Another friend references a journey:

> My Dear Margaret, Embarked on the stream of time—while prosperous gales waft you gaily and swiftly along, lighted with the bright, enchanting prospects on its banks, may this remind you of that star which will safely guide you in the ocean of eternity—the volume of Eternal Truth. Sometimes think of Martha S. M. Skilton.

Anne E. Hyde, Nathaniel Hyde's sister, and Margaret's sisters and her cousins both from her mother's and father's sides of the family are among the block signers.

Margaret's son, Thomas Locke Hyde, can be traced through federal census records. He enlisted in Company E, Massachusetts 39th Infantry Regiment, on August 12, 1862, and mustered out on March 9, 1865, at Washington, DC. He served as a butcher and prepared meat for the troops.

The quilt passed to Margaret's sister Ellen Maria Austin Locke, the youngest child of the family to live to adulthood. Ellen married James Swan of Dorchester, Massachusetts, and had seven children, the youngest of whom was the mother of the donor of the quilt to the Concord Museum, Concord, Massachusetts, in 1966.[17]

PORTLAND HALVES QUILT, 1843

Contributed by Debra Grana

Portland Halves Quilt, 1843. Made by the High Street Congregational Church Ladies' Society, Portland, Maine. Cotton, each half is 82" by 58". Collector Debra Grana found the two halves at a yard sale in upstate New York. Her research confirmed that the quilt was made for Reverend John Chickering and that the block contributors were wealthy women of the community. *Collection of Debra Grana*

Found at a village-wide yard sale in upstate New York, these quilt halves have been bound in woven tape that is different for each half; there are diagonal cuts in two inside corners (one on each quilt half) that have been crudely stitched back together. Why or when this quilt was cut in half remains a mystery.

Each cotton block is meticulously appliquéd or pieced (even by nine-year-old Mary G. Kelsey, whose block is inscribed with her age) and then quilted. Attached to one quilt half was a handwritten note: "Made by the High Street Congregational Church Ladies' Society for Rev. Chickering." Forty names are inked on the fronts and backs of the quilted blocks, with dates that range from August to December 1843 plus one for February 1845.

Sometimes quilts would be made for pastors as farewell gifts upon their reassignment to new churches or retirement, but Reverend John W. Chickering was the pastor of the High Street Congregational Church in Portland, Maine, from 1835 to 1865.[18] Perhaps it was an 1843 Christmas gift, with the later addition of the mystery 1845 date. While we do not know the event

Detail of the Portland Halves Quilt. *Photo by David Bohl*

for which the quilt was made for Reverend Chickering, the gift shows the high esteem his congregation had for him.

As with most coastal Maine towns, life in Portland revolved around the sea trade with the Carolinas and West Indies. Cargoes of lumber, ice, salted fish, furniture, and marine hardware sailed out of Portland in exchange for rum, molasses, and cotton. To accomplish all this required the building of ships in the numerous boatyards along the waterfront, thereby providing employment for those involved in shipbuilding and provisioning the ships.[19] Each of those individuals, as well as local businessmen, may have had an invested share of a particular ship, which gave them additional income from the cargo profits.[20] This made 1840s Portland very prosperous.

The women named on the quilt segments reflect this prosperity. Makers of the quilt blocks included the following:

Betsey and Sarah Lord, wife and daughter of the city treasurer;

Harriet and Harriet A. Kingsbury, wife and daughter of a hotelkeeper;

Mary C. Porter, wife of a papermaker (their daughter would marry Henry Wadsworth Longfellow's brother Andrew in 1852);

Harriet H. Mason, wife of an apothecary (Henrietta, their daughter, would marry the founder of International Paper Company in 1872);

Merrill Block, 1843. Dorcas Ellen Merrill, Portland, Maine. Cotton, 11" by 11". *Collection of Debra Grana; photo by Zephr Preservation Studio of Cohoes, New York*

Harriett Carter, wife of another apothecary;

Sarah Snow, widow of Nathaniel Snow, who had enlisted with the highly successful privateer USS *Dash* in January 1815 (the *Dash* was lost at sea during a gale just weeks later);

Harriet Thurston, wife of John Thurston, a shipbuilder and surveyor (Harriet was the daughter of Sarah and Nathaniel Snow and was born three months before her father's loss at sea); and

Eliza Chandler and Dorcas Ellen Merrill, both wives of ship masters.

MERRILL BLOCK, 1843

Contributed by Debra Grana

Several years after I acquired the 1843 Portland quilt halves, a single potholder block made by Dorcas Ellen Merrill came on the market. It is dated October 8, 1843, and inscribed "L. & D. E. Merrill, Portland," for Leonard and Dorcas Ellen Merrill. Unlike her simple but well-made sunflower block for the Portland halves quilt, this block is an oval motif cut from an 1825–35 English roller-printed fabric[21] that has been appliquéd to a background in the *broderie-perse* style. She removed the center of the motif (usually consisting of an eagle and shield or palmette leaf) to make room for her inked inscription.

Dorcas Ellen Gordon and Leonard W. Merrill were married by Rev. J. W. Chickering on September 22, 1841, so it isn't likely to have commemorated their anniversary. Whatever its reason for existence, this beautiful block is Dorcas's lasting legacy. In a few short years, scandal and tragedy would come to the family.

Dorcas was a Gordon by birth; she married into the Merrill family. Both families were longtime, successful seafaring merchants in Portland, Maine. Despite that, between 1852 and 1855, Leonard, Dorcas, and their children relocated to Chelsea, Massachusetts, leaving behind Dorcas's widowed mother and all their other relatives. Was this to expand the family seafaring opportunities? Or was this somehow related to the fact that on February 21, 1862, Nathaniel Gordon, Dorcas's younger brother, became "the only man in the history of the United States to be hanged for the crime of slave trading"?[22] Ten years later, at the age of fifty, Dorcas died of consumption (now known as tuberculosis).[23]

POMROY ALBUM QUILT, 1844

A dedicatory block is found near the center of an elegant silk potholder quilt in the collection of the Bangor Historical Society in Maine. The following words are printed, probably with a home printing press, on a fine cream-colored silk fabric, which was then quilted between the printed lines and bound in the same silk fabric.

> An offering of Friendship, from the Ladies of the First Church and Parish, to Mrs. Pomroy, Bangor May 30, 1844.
>
> "The Lord bless thee, and keep thee
>
> The Lord make his face shine upon thee, and be gracious unto thee;
>
> The Lord lift up his countenance upon thee, and give thee peace."

Ann Quincy Pomroy was the second wife of Swan Lyman Pomroy (also spelled Pomeroy), the minister of the First Church and Parish of Bangor, Maine, from 1825 to 1848. Ann Quincy married the reverend in 1835 in Portland, Maine. She was the daughter of Josiah Quincy and Nancy Bigelow of Portland.

As is too often the case, much can be found about Reverend Pomroy's history and his opinions on slavery, religion, and the need for a missionary society to spread the Lord's word, but there is no information about his wife beyond her birth, marriage, and death dates or why the quilt was made for her, beyond its quoted "offering of Friendship" in 1844. A 2011 article in the *Bangor Daily News* surmises that it was a parting gift, since Reverend Pomroy took a leave of absence to travel for a year and a half in Europe and Palestine, but that trip happened two years after the quilt was made.

The Reverend Swan Lyman Pomroy graduated from Brown University in 1820 and the Andover Theological Seminar four years later. In August 1825, he was ordained at the Bangor First Parish Church, and at his request he was dismissed in 1848, since he was appointed a

Pomroy Album Quilt, 1844. Presented by the Ladies of the First Church and Parish, Bangor, Maine. Silk, wool, 68" by 43". Made for Ann Quincy Pomroy, wife of Swan Lyman Pomroy, as a friendship offering. Many of the blocks are meticulously embroidered in silk or wool, and two blocks are painted by the artist Mary Ann Hardy. *Courtesy of the Bangor Historical Society, Bangor, Maine; gift of Mrs. Isabel Wales, 76.A*

Dedicatory block for Mrs. Pomroy from the Ladies of the First Church and Parish. *Courtesy of the Bangor Historical Society, Bangor, Maine; gift of Mrs. Isabel Wales, 76.A*

A view of the second First Church, ca. 1860. *Courtesy of the Bangor Historical Society*

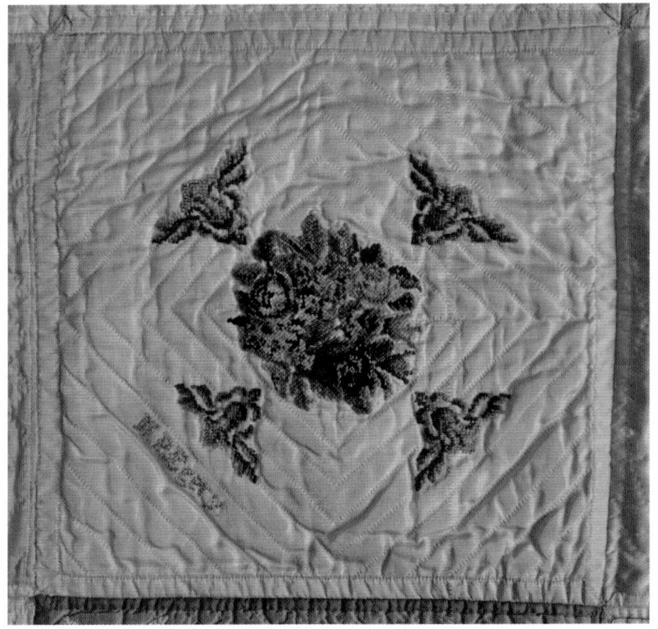

Pomroy Album Quilt detail of embroidered quilt block, wool on silk, by M. P. Egery. *Courtesy of the Bangor Historical Society, Bangor, Maine; gift of Mrs. Isabel Wales, 76.A*

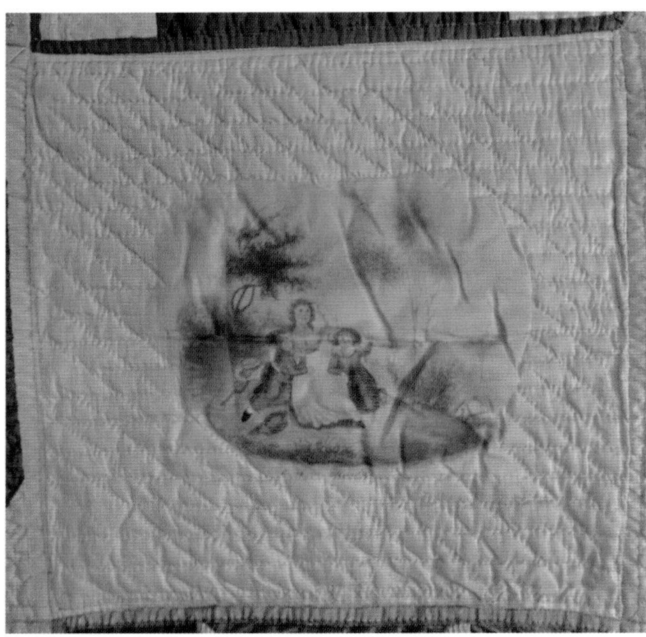

Pomroy Album Quilt detail of block painted by Mary Ann Hardy. *Courtesy of the Bangor Historical Society, Bangor, Maine; gift of Mrs. Isabel Wales, 76.A*

corresponding secretary of the American Board of Commissioners of Foreign Missions. He campaigned in favor of international Christian missions, preached for temperance, and was nationally known for his work to end slavery.

Only one child from six pregnancies in ten years survived from his first marriage, to Frances Maria Fales, daughter of a prominent Taunton, Massachusetts, lawyer and judge. Their daughter Mary Barnes Pomroy was born about 1831, married the Reverend Orlando Henry White in 1852, and died childless in 1855.

Pomroy's second marriage, to Ann Quincy, yielded another daughter, Anne Louisa, who also married a clergyman, the Reverend Ephraim Cummings, and they are recorded as childless in the *Cummings Family Genealogy* (1888). I can find no relationship between the Pomroy family and the donor of the quilt, Isabel Wales, who gave it in 1964.

In total, there are forty elegantly made 9-inch silk squares signed by thirty-four makers. Three women made more than one block, three signatures are damaged or undecipherable, and the dedication block is unsigned. A block made in memory of Mrs. Mary H. P. Walker, embroidered in elegant black-and-white floral motifs wound into a wreath, is also unsigned. The signers range in age from seventeen to sixty-nine years old, most of them members of the church. Mary and Sophia Stackpole were dressmakers, Mrs. Ruth Ingraham was a widow and milliner, and several other women were the wives of prominent Bangor merchants.

Many blocks are worked in wool or silk threads in crewel, cross-stitch, or half-cross-stitch embroidery. There are several patchwork and appliquéd blocks, including star and Puss in the Corner patterns. Some of the blocks are signed in ink, some have embroidered signatures, and some are lettered with a homestyle printing kit. The work in several blocks is exceptionally fine, with tiny stitches in the embroidery and quilting that measure twenty stitches to the inch.

Two of the blocks contain painted scenes and are attributed to Mary Ann Hardy (1809–1887), a noted Bangor-area artist who specialized in watercolor portraits painted on ivory. She was the sister and student of Jeremiah Pearson Hardy, who was much sought after for his portraits in the mid-nineteenth century. He painted a portrait of her as a young girl that is in the collection of the Boston Museum of Fine Arts.

The western bank of the Penobscot River, where Bangor is situated, was an important meeting place for Native Americans and had a permanent European settlement called Kenduskeag Plantation by 1790. It was renamed and incorporated as a town in 1791. Bangor sits 60 miles from the Atlantic Ocean, but thanks to the navigable depth of the Penobscot River, it became the self-proclaimed timber capital of the world by 1850. Many families became wealthy through exporting timber from Maine's forests or in the shipbuilding industry.

Portrait of a Young Child, 1853. Mary Ann Hardy, Maine. Watercolor on ivory, gold, clear stones. Overall, 2⅞" by 1½". Miniatures painted by Mary Ann Hardy are held in several museum collections; this example was sold at auction in 2015. The case is engraved on the reverse "S. L. Dyer / Brewer, Me / 1853." *Northeast Auctions, Portsmouth, New Hampshire*

Mary Ann Hardy, 1821. Jeremiah Pearson Hardy, Maine. Oil on panel. Jeremiah Hardy painted his sister Mary Ann when she was twelve years old and he was at the beginning of his career. He became a well-respected portraitist, and the Bangor Historical Association holds several of his later works. *Museum of Fine Arts, Boston; gift of Mazim Karolik for the M. and M. Karolik Collection of American Paintings, 1815–1865, 47.1135*

The Bangor waterfront, showing the second First Church on the far side of the Penobscot River, ca. 1860. *Courtesy of the Bangor Historical Society*

SARAH A. LEAVITT QUILT, 1847

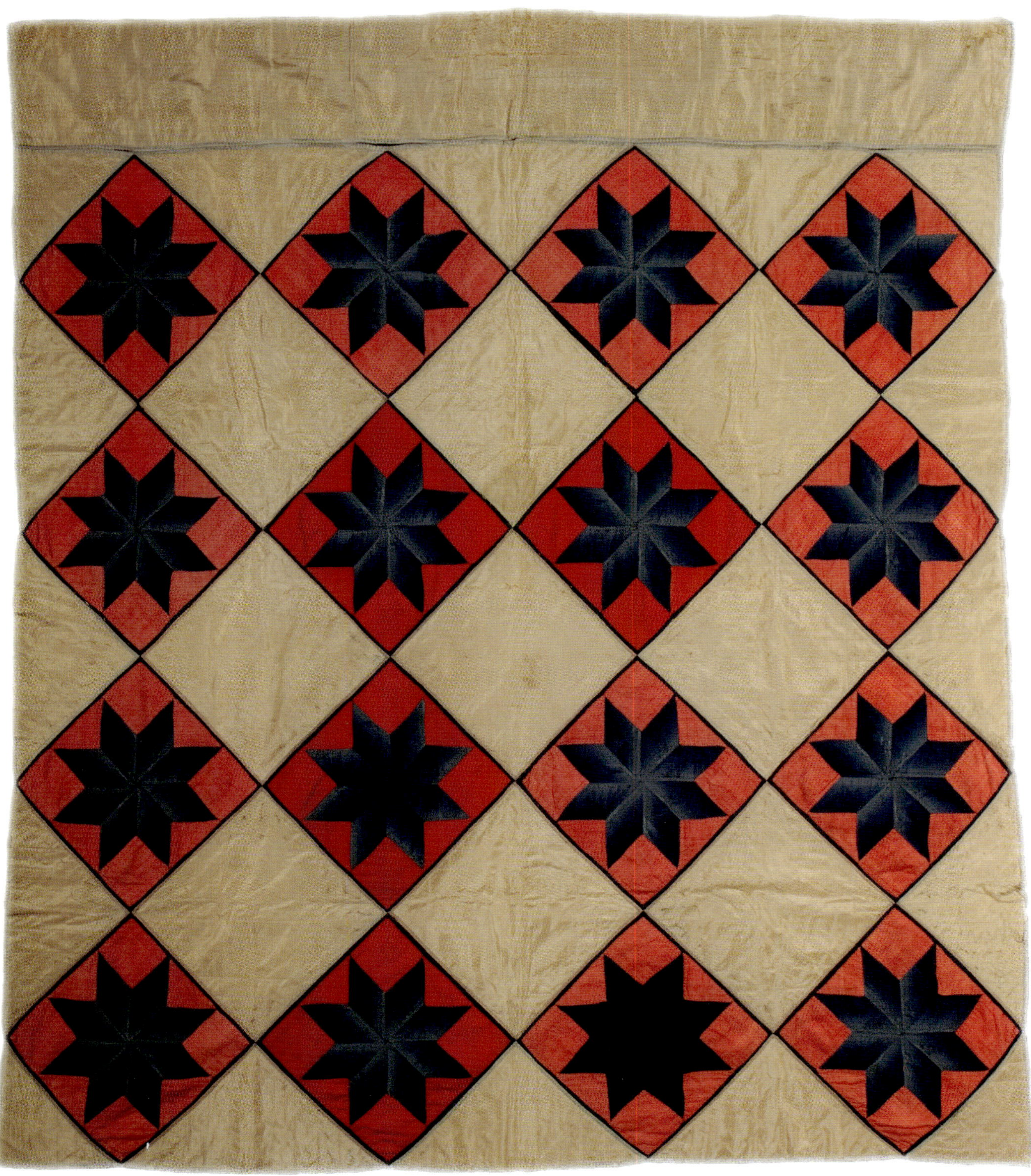

Sarah A. Leavitt Quilt, 1847. Sarah A. Leavitt, Manchester, New Hampshire. Silk and cotton, 64" by 58". A quilt constructed of individually finished blocks, this is the first quilt the author purchased and the one that set this quest in motion. *Collection of the author; photo by David Bohl*

Detail, Sarah A. Leavitt Quilt. *Photo by David Bohl*

Detail of the Sarah A. Leavitt Quilt in which the red cotton has been pulled back to show the bright-pink silk beneath

The purchase at auction of the Sarah A. Leavitt quilt changed my life. I did not expect it to start what became a twenty-year search for the origin of an unusually constructed style of quilt, culminating in two books (one on Civil War quilts), but that is what evolved. I love inscribed quilts and seek those that include the names of any of my forebears, and I was certain that Sarah A. Leavitt was one of them—my great-great-grandmother who lived in Loudon, New Hampshire. The search for the source of instructions for block-by-block quilts (with training from many mentors) led me to a deep interest in quilt history, women's history, and the history of my native New England.

I now know three things for certain: a silk quilt with the name "Sarah A. Leavitt" and the date "December 16, 1847" was meticulously stitched and carefully embroidered; this quilt was sold out of the estate of Marian Hill Hoyt of Manchester, New Hampshire, in 2000; and Sarah A. Leavitt was *not* my great-great-grandmother. I assume Sarah made the quilt, but I am not certain which Sarah A. Leavitt made my silk quilt, so the story I am weaving here is a deeply researched theory at best. The search has been fun, educational, and exhaustive.

From the beginning I have based my theory on geography. There were Sarah A. Leavitts in the Manchester area at the time this quilt was made. My research revealed several more geographical coincidences and possible connections between the assumed maker's families and those of the woman who possessed the quilt when she died in 2000.

I started my search for Sarah A. Leavitt in the New Hampshire Historical Society (NHHS) research library. The quilt is dated 1847, and Sarah may have been between fifteen and twenty-five years old when she made it. With this date range, I began searching for a Sarah A. Leavitt who would have been born between 1822 and 1832. To my dismay, I discovered that there were fourteen young women in just one of six published Leavitt genealogies held by the NHHS with the first name Sarah and the middle initial "A" born in that date range. They lived all over New England. I read through the entries in this book and five other Leavitt genealogies and searched to see if the date embroidered on the quilt was related to any event meaningful to the women listed in these books, but I found none.[24]

Concurrently, I began to research the source of the quilt. It was purchased in the auction of the household goods of Marion Hill Hoyt, who was born in Manchester, New Hampshire, in 1900, lived there all of her life, and died in 2000. In an amazing coincidence, a year after acquiring the quilt at auction, I evaluated some quilts for Marion's daughter-in-law, June Hoyt. In the process, we discussed Marion Hoyt, her penchant for collecting, and the three generations of family goods sold in that auction. June said that the home where Marion lived had been in the family since the 1870s, and that she was the third generation to live on what was once the second home and farm of Marion's wealthy grandfather Bushrod Washington Hill.[25]

I narrowed my search to the Sarah A. Leavitts who were living in or near Manchester at the time the quilt was made. Searching the Manchester city directories in the collection of the Manchester Historic Association, which covered every other year from 1844 into the 1960s, I found one Sarah in the directory of 1844, none in 1846, and two in 1848.[26]

I chose as my quilt maker a young woman who was boarding with Mrs. Mary Brown in 1846 and who, along with Mrs. Brown, was listed as a dressmaker. This choice is based partially on the silk used in the quilt—it is a fine weight such as was used in dressmaking, and it was a popular color of the time. The blue stars are pieced of ribbons woven with images of birds, with the exception of one block pieced in a navy-blue damask—materials easily available to a dressmaker.

As I continued my research into the Leavitts and the two families into which Sarah married (the Noyes and the Perry families) and Marion's families (the Hoyt and Hill families), more possible connections among the five families emerged, but they were enough only to strengthen, not prove, my suppositions.

Manchester, New Hampshire, became one of the largest manufacturing centers in the world, with rapid development and growth in the mid-nineteenth century. The area chosen for development is located on the Merrimack River where it cascades over a series of falls and rapids, dropping 50 feet in a very short distance, providing abundant potential waterpower. The earliest mills were built on the western side of the river before the American Revolution and processed wood and grains. Here, cotton was spun by waterpower as early as 1810, and the first large company was named the Amoskeag Cotton and Woolen Manufacturing Company. Development spread rapidly to the eastern side of the river, and hundreds of dwelling places were built for the mill operatives.[27] The 1850 Manchester city directory notes the exploding census figures decade by decade: from 557 residents in 1800, to 887 in 1830, to 3,234 in 1840, and to 15,500 in 1850.

Thousands of women and men moved to Manchester from towns all over northern New England for employment in the mills and to service a fast-growing urban population.[28] By midcentury, European immigrants joined the influx. Women came to be trained as mill operatives, and some men trained to be machinists. Farmers, grocers, dressmakers, shopkeepers, and horse wranglers came hoping to make a living during the growth of the new city.

The families in this narrative removed primarily from three towns. Several members of Sewell Leavitt's family (Sarah A.'s father) moved from Meredith, in Belknap County, including his brother and brother-in-law. The Perrys and the Noyeses are the two families into which Sarah married, and they originated in Grafton and Orange, neighboring towns in Grafton

View of the Stark Mills from the West Bank of the Merrimack River, ca. 1855. Luthy, Manchester, New Hampshire. Oil on canvas, 25" by 35½". Sarah Leavitt is listed in the Manchester city directory as an operative in the Stark Mills. *Courtesy of the Manchester Historical Association, 1994.007.002*

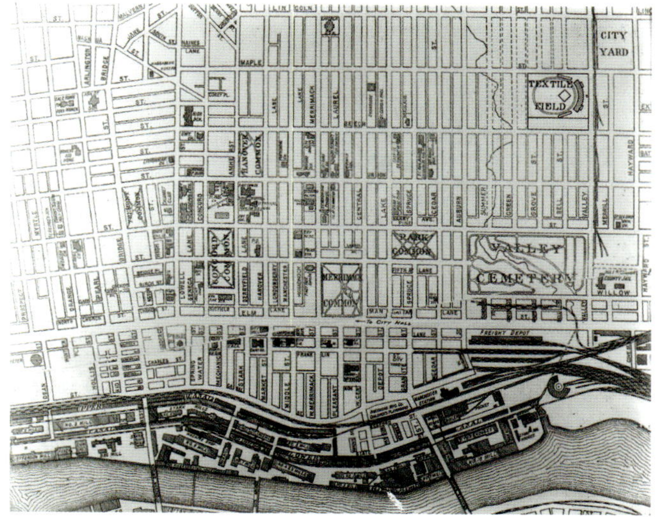

Map of the Mill Yards and Housing, ca. 1913, Manchester, New Hampshire. The map shows many of the mills and the proximity of the mill yard housing. Sarah A. Leavitt worked in the Stark Mills and lived in the Stark housing. *Courtesy of the Manchester Historical Association, 1913 MHAGN 228*

A View of Manchester, New Hampshire, 1855, from a painting by John B. Bachelder. Lithograph. The lovely bucolic scene shows the development of Manchester on the east side of the Merrimack River, and the farms and houses spreading eastward as the city grew. *Courtesy of the Yale University Art Gallery, 1946.9.1767*

County. The Hills and Hoyts, who were Marion Hill Hoyt's families, also came from Grafton, New Hampshire.

Sarah Ann Leavitt was born in Meredith, New Hampshire, in 1826, the oldest of three children, including Nancy and Josiah. Her mother was Hannah Bell Fogg, and her father, Sewell Leavitt, moved the family to Manchester before 1837 (Josiah was born in Manchester in that year). The family is listed in Manchester in the 1840 federal census. The five family members are listed only by age—Sarah and Nancy were the two females between ten and fourteen of age. One family member was employed in the mills; this could have been Sarah, at age fourteen.

Sewell was a butcher and is listed in this occupation in the Manchester city directories and the federal census from 1844 through the 1860s. He died in 1870. He appears in several sources that document early Manchester history; he was elected to the first common council in 1846, later called aldermen, and he served three consecutive two-year terms.[29] He then served a two-year term (1851–1853) in the New Hampshire House of Representatives. In a Manchester Water Works survey map of 1856, his farm property is shown in Hallsville, a village on the east side of Manchester, on the map next to that of this brother J. Leavitt and his nephew J. L. Fogg.

In the 1848 city directory (usually enumerated in January as stated in the introduction of the publication), a Sarah Leavitt is boarding in the residence of Mary Jones, dressmaker, and is a dressmaker herself. The residence is in the Central Block of housing, between Stark and Mechanic Streets, home to many of the mill workers. Sarah is recorded as working in the Stark Corporation, which was within a block of her residence. If this is our Sarah, it would not be unusual for her to board out away from her family, since the mill shifts were long, up to eleven hours per day, with only half-hour breaks for meals.[30] Her family home was more than a mile and a half from the Stark Mills, and it would have been impossible for her to run home for meals.

Sarah married Joseph Noyes on May 14, 1848 (just five months after the date on the quilt), with the ceremony officiated by Cyrus W. Wallace, pastor of the Congregational Church. Joseph Noyes died of consumption, as tuberculosis was called at the time, on January 14, 1850, and their son, Stephen, was born ten weeks later on March 30. In the 1850 census, Sarah and her son, Stephen J. Noyes, are living on the farm of her father, Sewell, a butcher, with her mother, Hannah, and her siblings, Josiah, age twelve, and Nancy E., twenty. The farm was valued by the census taker at $4,000—nearly twice the average value of the properties in the area. Sewell Leavitt was a prosperous farmer and butcher, providing food for the exploding population.

Five years later, on August 27, 1855, Sarah married Matthew Newell Perry, a teamster born in 1831, whose parents moved to Manchester from Grafton, New Hampshire. There is an interesting entry in the 1854 report of the City of Manchester, Division of Highways and Bridges, District 7. Sewell Leavitt and several Perrys were paid for labor. Could this be a connection between the families that would result in the marriage between Sarah and Matthew Newell Perry? The Manchester city directory at this time lists both families living near each other in Hallsville, a neighborhood east of the Manchester city center. Sarah and Matthew had three children; the oldest, Jeff T. Perry, was born in Orange, New Hampshire, a small village next to Grafton. Matthew died of consumption at the age of thirty-six on December 2, 1867; Sarah had just turned forty-one years old. In 1869, she appears on a list of paupers in Manchester. The 1870 census lists Sarah as the head of a household of six people: Sarah, age forty-four; Joseph, twenty-one (on the railroad); Ursula, fourteen; Jeffie, eleven; and Josiah Perry, seventy-five (her father-in-law, who passed away later that year). Her youngest child, Emma, was presumably living with her as well.

Members of the Hill and Hoyt families moved to Manchester from Orange and Grafton, New Hampshire. The Hill brothers came first, and by 1850 John Hill, the eldest of three who came to Manchester, established an express business that eventually took trade between Manchester, New Hampshire, and Lawrence and Boston, Massachusetts. It was taken over by Bushrod Washington Hill, the youngest of the family entrepreneurs and the grandfather of Marion Hill Hoyt. Bushrod became a prominent business leader in the city, served on the boards of banks, and eventually sold the Hill Express Company to American Express.[31]

Bushrod died in 1913, and in his will he left his estate in trust, leaving the use of his home on Hanover Street to his wife, and a farm at the corner of Old Bridge Street and Mammoth Road to his son John Franklin Hill, Marion's father.[32] This property became the home of Marion Hill and her husband, Edward E. Hoyt.

The Hoyt family came to Manchester later than the other families and do not appear in the Manchester city directories until the late 1870s. Moses Hoyt is listed as a fruit peddler, and his son Edward E. (born in Orange, New Hampshire, in 1868) as a teamster, driving horses. In 1892, Edward married Flora Knights and established a livery, where horses could be stabled or rented. After Edward's death in 1916, Flora continued the business and was listed in the city directories as a horse dealer. Their son Elmer W. Hoyt worked in the family horse business, which he transformed into Hoyt's Riding School in the 1920s, and it operated into the 1960s. He married Marion Atwood Hill, granddaughter of Bushrod,

Advertisement from the Manchester city directory, 1860, Manchester, New Hampshire. Bushrod Washington Hill came to Manchester in the 1850s, joined his brother in the express business, and bought out other partners. The Sarah A. Leavitt quilt was sold out of the estate of his granddaughter Marion Hill Hoyt. *Courtesy of the Manchester Historical Association*

in 1918, and the directories continue to list the family living on the Hill farm.

Sarah A. Perry, widow of Matthew N., continued to be listed in the city directories as a dressmaker until two years before her death in 1913. Her daughter Ursula remains in Manchester with the same occupation as her mother—dressmaker. The directories list both Ursula and her younger sister Emma, also a dressmaker, boarding with Sarah.

Tracing the quilt's change of ownership relies on speculation. Did Matthew Perry, Sarah's second husband, work for Hill Express Company as a teamster? When he died, leaving Sarah with three young children, did she sell some of her household goods and her quilt to the Hill family, perhaps to raise some much-needed cash? The Hills were wealthy enough for Bushrod's wife and daughters to afford dressmakers. Did they employ Sarah Perry or her daughters, thus making another business connection? The census records for 1910 show the Perrys and the Bushrod Hill family living just a block apart in Manchester. Did Ursula Perry sell the quilt to the Hoyt family after her mother's death? Or perhaps Marion Hill Hoyt picked it up at an auction of the Perry family goods after Ursula died in 1922. We will never know, but the research has provided enough hints for me to weave a story of five families whose lives certainly connected in a fast-growing New Hampshire mill city.

PARIS HILL FRIENDSHIP QUILT, 1848

Paris Hill Friendship Quilt, 1848. Made by members of the Baptist Church of Paris Hill, Maine, for Louisa Griffin Davis, wife of the minister. Cotton, silk, velvet, 101" by 101". *Hamlin Memorial Library and Museum; photo by Mike Taylor*

Hamlin Memorial Hall, Paris Hill, Maine. Once a jail for Oxford County, Maine, it now houses a public library and museum. *Courtesy of the Hamlin Memorial Library and Museum*

Paris Hill Baptist Church, Paris Hill, Maine

The Hamlin Memorial Library and Museum in Paris Hill, Maine, is housed in what began as the jail for Oxford County, Maine. One of four buildings constructed for county business, it was built in 1822 and remained the jail until 1896, when new county buildings were built in South Paris, closer to the railroad. The stone structure was purchased by Dr. Augustus C. Hamlin, nephew of Hannibal Hamlin (US vice president during the first term of President Abraham Lincoln, 1856–1860). Augustus performed extensive renovations to the building and then donated it to the Paris Hill Library Association; his stipulations included naming the building Hamlin Hall.[33] The small lending library is housed on the first floor, and on the second floor is a museum that interprets the history of Paris Hill and its citizens.

An elegant inscribed variety quilt constructed block by block is placed on display in the museum each summer. Its sixty-one full blocks and twenty half blocks were pieced, appliquéd, or embroidered and then inscribed by women of the village in 1848. Most of the blocks are made of cotton, but there are also blocks with silk and plush appliqué, and one of the blocks has a cross embroidered with the quilter's hair. Every block is bound in a Prussian blue print, and the blocks are whipstitched together. The quilt was presented to Louisa Griffin Davis, wife of the second minister of the Paris Hill Baptist Church, which still sits across the common from Hamlin Hall.

The seventy-two signers of the quilt blocks were parishioners of this church and included women and one man from all levels of Paris Hill and South Paris society. There are several family groups, sisters, a brother, mothers, cousins, and neighbors. The signers included the wives of physicians and lawyers; a woman who later served as a nurse during the Civil War; and the mother, sisters, and first and second wives of Hannibal Hamlin.

Persis Sibley Andrews was one of the block makers. She was the daughter of William Sibley and Charlotte Buxton Sibley of Freedom, Maine. Her father and his brothers founded Freedom and were part of the second wave of settlers to come from well-educated families in Massachusetts at the end of the eighteenth century. Persis Sibley was sent to Miss Murray's School for Young Ladies in Hallowell, Maine, where her education ranged from the classics to household crafts. The Maine Historical Society in Portland has several items she made, including a painted fire screen and lace cuffs and collars.[34]

Sibley taught school, read and studied voraciously, and enjoyed an active social life. She read all of Shakespeare's plays one year and attended lectures on chemistry and other subjects. Sibley had a lifelong interest in arts, education, and politics. She was an avid diarist and kept descriptive accounts of her experiences and views. "I take too much interest in legislation for a lady," she once wrote. In 1839, she wrote that life was so pleasant without marriage that she liked being an old maid. But that didn't stop her from marrying Charles Andrews ("the handsomest lawyer in Augusta") on June 22, 1842, when she was twenty-eight years old.[35] Andrews studied law with the honorable Hannibal Hamlin and was appointed attorney for Oxford County, requiring the couple to move to Paris Hill.

Persis Sibley Andrews kept her diary for many years, entering local and national news items, reports on the health of family members, and comments on village life. Her diary entry from August 13, 1848, is the earliest known reference to block-by-block quilts:

> I have at last made my square to Mrs. Davis Album Quilt & it is really beautiful. It contains all the work I have done in the week beside family cares (my baby has not been well) & is only one foot square quilted & bound. I do not approve of this way of making a quilt for the Ministers wife, but I have a great deal of esteem & admiration for the lady & beside wishing to be remembered by her I wish to see the variety quilt finished as it wanted only half a dozen of the required 70 before I made mine.[36]

Miniature Portrait of Persis Sibley Andrews and Daughter, 1844. Miss Wardell, Dixfield, Maine. Watercolor on ivory, 2¾" by 2½". Diarist Persis Sibley Andrews wrote on February 22, 1844, "Miss Wardell—a Miniature painter is here & she excels in her art, if I am a judge." The child pictured was her eldest daughter, Charlotte Buxton Andrews, born in 1843. *Collection of the Maine Historical Society, #271*

Detail, Paris Hill Friendship Quilt. The center block with the blue star was made by Persis Sibley Andrews. *Courtesy of the Hamlin Memorial Library and Museum*

Her daughter, Persis Nevins Andrews, donated the quilt to the Maine Historical Society in the 1930s. A newspaper article from 1933 explains the donation:

> About thirty years ago Mrs. Thayer (formerly Mrs. Davis) gave the quilt to Miss P. N. Andrews, then a resident of Paris Hill, with the comment that the square most admired for nicety and variety of work, was made by Miss A's mother. Her name, Persis Sibley Andrews, in delicate script, is perfectly eligible today. When the second owner of the quilt removed from Paris, she gave it to Hamlin Memorial Hall for safe keeping.

Detail, Paris Hill Friendship Quilt. Note the embroidery and signature of Persis Sibley Andrews. *Courtesy of the Hamlin Memorial Library and Museum; photo by Mike Taylor*

This was once the Paris Hill home of Persis Sibley Andrews and family.

Detail, Paris Hill Friendship Quilt. The figure in this block is cut from a textile printed with President John Adams, who died on July 4, 1826. *Courtesy of the Hamlin Memorial Library and Museum; photo by Mike Taylor*

GALLERY OF QUILTS

Raffle Quilt, 1852. Various makers, Portsmouth, New Hampshire. Silk, 78" by 62". Ninety-nine 7" blocks of silk are finely quilted and finished knife edge. The quilt was made to raise funds for a Portsmouth church, but instead of signing the blocks, names on slips of paper were attached to the reverse for later execution. The winner took the quilt away, but the inscriptions were never finished. *Courtesy of the Portsmouth Historical Society; photo by David Bohl*

Detail of the 1852 Raffle Quilt. *Courtesy of the Portsmouth Historical Society; photo by David Bohl*

East Dennis Friendship Quilt, ca. 1840. Various makers, East Dennis, Massachusetts. Cotton, 100" by 98". The blocks are set on point, and many of the triangular half blocks on the edges are made of preprinted patchwork. Six pairs of blocks of identical pattern run down the central axis of the quilt. The repeated patterns include hearts and interlinked circles, leading previous historians to assume it was made as a wedding quilt. *Courtesy of the Dennis (MA) Historical Society, J 1505*

Detail of East Dennis Friendship Quilt, showing cutout corners to fit a four-poster bed and the preprinted patchwork half squares at the edges. *Courtesy of the Dennis (MA) Historical Society, J 1505*

CHAPTER 4

FRIENDSHIP AND PRESENTATION QUILTS 1851–1860

Research points to the central coast of Maine as the epicenter of potholder quilts. Several researchers are studying a group of friendship and presentation quilts made in Cumberland County, with a remarkably large number made in the town of Center Cumberland. The following essay outlines what has been discovered as of summer 2019.

THE ALBUM QUILTS OF CENTER CUMBERLAND, MAINE

Contributed by Laureen LaBar

Incorporated in 1821, Cumberland, Maine, is a town of rich farmland, with a small slice of coast on Casco Bay making up its southern boundary. The village at the heart of the town is called Cumberland Center. Through the late 1800s, many of the men of the town were involved in maritime trades as captains, seamen, brokers, traders, and shipbuilders. Maine's state seal features a farmer and a mariner, and the two industries had comparable representation in Cumberland in the mid-1800s.[37] Town histories read like lists of ship captains, and many more men filled less prestigious posts at sea. The mariners were absent from home for months and even years at a time. Cumberland's wives, all but absent from the annals of the town, ran households and farms, kept the books, and supported the churches, schools, and libraries.

In 1831, a year of religious revivals, the Cumberland Center Congregational Church was built in the heart of the town.[38] This church was the spiritual home of many of the town's ship captains, although their wives' and daughters' names appear on the church rolls more often than theirs. Many of these women participated in the church's Ladies' Sewing Circle, which constructed ten quilts between 1849 and circa 1855.[39]

Cumberland Center Community Church, Cumberland Center, Maine

The locations of nine of the ten mid-nineteenth-century Cumberland Center Congregational Church Ladies' Sewing Circle (C4) quilts are known, and the quilts have been examined.[40] Eight were constructed using the potholder method. The quilts contain many common blocks and fabrics. They have a large number of inscribed names in common and appear to have been made for people at the heart of the community. The *Bark Messenger* quilt of 1850 is the largest of these quilts. Its ninety-seven blocks are inscribed with sixty-four names. It appears to have been made for a person, couple, or family that was leaving the community for Massachusetts. A central block, for which the quilt has been named, bears an embroidered ship with the inscription "The Bark Messenger laden with friendship, bound for Wellfleet."

Bark Messenger Quilt, 1850. Ladies Sewing Circle of the Cumberland Center Congregational Church, Cumberland Center, Maine. Cotton, 99" by 108". One of several quilts made by the Ladies Sewing Circle between 1849 and about 1855. There are sixty-four inscribed names. *Courtesy of the Maine State Museum, 2011.36.1; photo by Mike Taylor*

Ladies Sewing Circle Quilt, Ladies Sewing Circle of the Cumberland Center Congregational Church, 1852, Cumberland Center, Maine. Cotton, silk, wool, 90" by 84". A paper label sewn to the back states, "Made by the Ladies Sewing Circle, Cumberland Center, 1852." The quilt contains elaborately embroidered blocks, and there are twenty-eight inscribed names but no indication of its purpose. *Courtesy of Quilts, Inc., Houston, Texas, 2010.06; photo by Jim Lincoln, Austin, Texas*

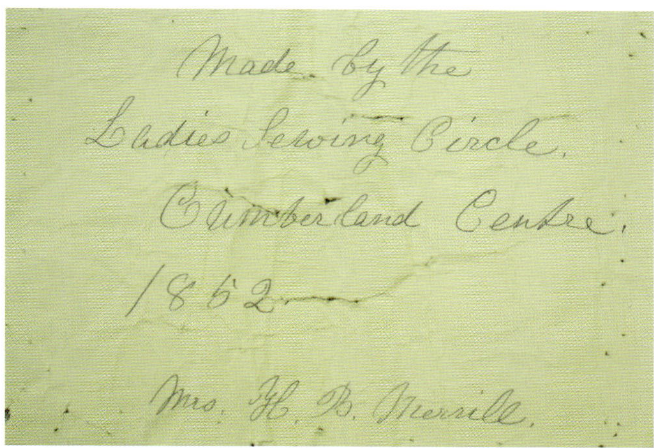

Detail of the note attached to the back of the Ladies Sewing Circle Quilt

The Ladies Sewing Circle Quilt displays the most elegant embroidery of any of this group of quilts.

Detail of the Ladies Sewing Circle Quilt. Many of the Cumberland Center Community Church quilts have block and embroidery patterns that repeat on other quilts.

A year later, Mrs. H. B. (Hannah Blanchard) Merrill made a block in another of the group's quilts. She became its owner and attached a note stating that it was "Made by the Ladies Sewing Circle. Cumberland Center. 1852," prompting the authors to dub it the LSC quilt. Twenty-eight names are inscribed on its blocks. The reason for its creation is not known.

The Lyre quilt is undated, but it was most likely made around the same time as the LSC, Bark Messenger, and other quilts, since they share blocks, appliqué motifs, and inscribed names. Some of the imagery on the Lyre quilt differs from other C4 quilts; its makers appliquéd images of household tools and dishes around the perimeter. The quilt includes few inscriptions, and those speak of or imply loss. It may have been made to commemorate the death of someone close to one of the group members.

Lyre Quilt, ca. 1850. Ladies Sewing Circle of the Cumberland Center Congregational Church, Cumberland Center, Maine. Cotton, silk, wool, 83" by 76½". Several blocks repeat patterns and embroidery motifs from other C4 quilts. Note the use of images of things found in the home—such as a butter churn, mantel clock, and wood stove implements. *Courtesy of Historic New England; gift of Miss Lola B. Tomlinson, 1968.6*

Detail of the Lyre Quilt. Another example of an embroidery pattern found in several of the Cumberland Center quilts.

The occasion for the construction of most of the other C4 quilts is unknown. Family tradition says that the Comet quilt was made for the 1849 marriage of Lucy Sweetser and Davis Merrill. The Jane Blanchard quilt was ostensibly made in honor of her wedding, but she was married twenty years before the quilt was made. The recipients of some quilts are known: in 1851 the group gave Captain Wilson his namesake quilt. They gave a quilt to Mary Ellen Wyman Merrill the same year, and another to a member of the Sweetser family around that time.

More than 200 names appear on the C4 quilts. Of these, twelve are male family members (ten husbands, two sons), and at least two are very young daughters (twins), all of whom were unlikely to have made the blocks that bear their names. These blocks and many others were inscribed, not signed. While this generally prevents identification of the maker of a particular block, it also suggests that the featured individual was important to the quilt's recipient and to the community of Cumberland Center.

In 1857, the ladies of the Poland Corner Methodist Church in Cumberland Center made a quilt. The Methodist and Congregational Churches are less than 3 miles apart. Despite their proximity, none of the women from the Congregational Church appear to have participated in the Poland Corner quilt. Differences in religious belief might explain why neighborliness did not extend to quilt making. However, this behavior extends beyond the hamlet of Cumberland Center and seems unrelated to religious beliefs. Only seven of the 200 names appearing on C4 quilts have been found on a sample of fourteen other Cumberland County quilts from the third quarter of the 1800s. The seven seem to have been on the periphery of the C4 sewing circle. Of them, only one name, that of Jane Merrill, is present on more than one of the C4 quilts. Her name appears on the two quilts with the largest number of names and, thus, the largest social sweep. Twenty years later, Merrill's name appears again on a quilt from West Falmouth, a town adjacent to Cumberland. It seems that the Cumberland Center's Congregational Church Ladies' Sewing Circle made quilts only for members of their church community.

Captain Wilson Quilt, 1851. Ladies Sewing Circle of the Cumberland Center Congregational Church, Cumberland Center, Maine. Cotton, silk, 88" by 62". Some of the motifs are found in other Cumberland Center quilts. This quilt also has unique ones, including the captain's home and unusual floral arrangements. *Courtesy of the Cumberland Historical Society, 97.1*

The block depicting Captain Wilson's home on the Captain Wilson Quilt. *Courtesy of the Cumberland Historical Society, 97.1*

Captain Wilson's home was across the street from the Cumberland Center Community Church, and today it appears much as it did on a block in his quilt.

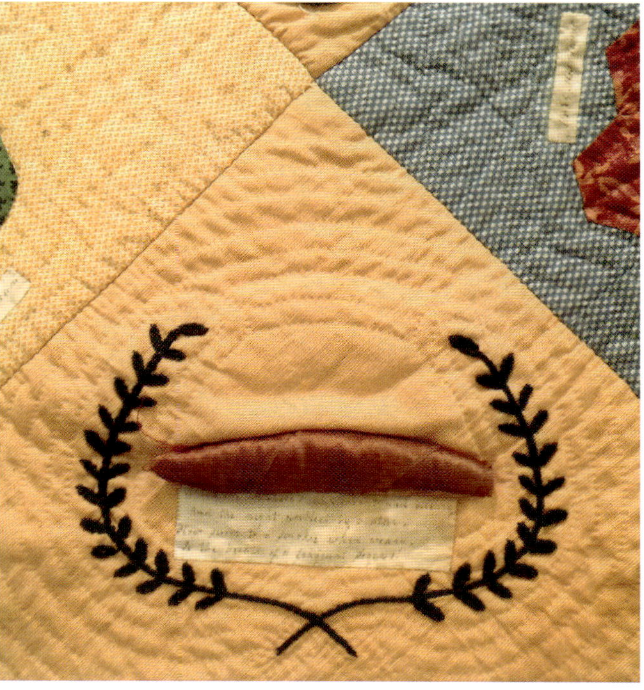

Captain Wilson Quilt, detail of the cigar block. "When the weather's unpleasant and dreary, And the night unblest by a star, How sweet to a smoker when weary, Is the breath of a fragrant cigar!"

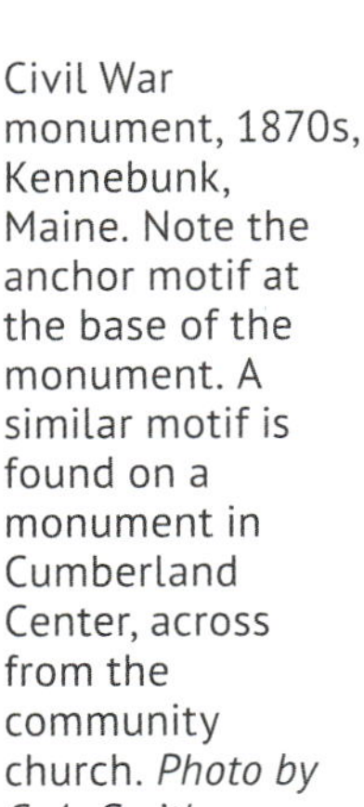

Civil War monument, 1870s, Kennebunk, Maine. Note the anchor motif at the base of the monument. A similar motif is found on a monument in Cumberland Center, across from the community church. *Photo by C. A. Smith*

Detail of the Captain Wilson Quilt

Detail of quilt block, showing "hope" embroidered near an appliquéd anchor

Detail of the Civil War Album Quilt. Both Munjoy Hill Civil War quilts have anchor blocks.

In the five years from 1849 to 1853, these ladies made nine or ten quilts for members of their small community. Six were made between 1849 and 1851 and one in 1852. One C4 quilt may have been made in the early 1840s, and no other quilts have been found dating between 1853 and the 1870s, when a younger generation of Sewing Circle members made at least two quilts. Reasons for discontinuing their efforts are not known, but the possibilities are many. Making two or more quilts a year is an ambitious exercise, and without the energy of a determined and capable organizer or team, success is not assured. Any number of minor events could have derailed the process: the health of organizers may have been compromised, quilters might have had to give their attention to raising children or assisting family members, or a community need could have arisen, shifting the energy and direction of the group. Solomon and Huldah Blanchard, whose names appear on the Bark Messenger quilt, died in September 1852, eleven days apart. Eight other town residents also died that fall. This followed another cluster of deaths in the spring of 1853.[41] Events such these would have required the attention and time of many family members and neighbors in the town's small quilting community. More quilts of the Cumberland Center Congregational Church Ladies' Sewing Circle may be found, and we may come to better understand the community, the reasons the quilts were made, and why the women stopped making them.

—Laureen LaBar

FISHERVILLE FRIENDSHIP QUILT

Fisherville Friendship Quilt, ca. 1860. Various makers, New Hampshire. Cotton, 86" by 88". The inscriptions on this quilt include Bible references and marital advice. *Private collection; photo by David Bohl*

The fad for making inscribed quilts peaked in the mid-nineteenth century and into the Civil War era. They range from small and humble repeating-block quilts to large appliquéd and embroidered masterpieces. Fisherville Friendship quilt has sixty-four 10-inch blocks that are pieced in the snowflake or album block pattern, one of the most common blocks used for inscribed quilts in this time period. Four stout arms extend to the corners of the block from an inscribed center square.

The blocks are bound with a medium-value, double-blue (blue printed over blue) print, set on point, and the makers chose to use the same double-blue fabric to make the isosceles triangle setting blocks required to achieve straight sides on the quilt. The blocks are carefully arranged: those with the brightest-yellow and deepest-red patches are near the center, and some of the blocks with the darkest fabrics are found along the top and bottom of the quilt. Corners are left out at the right and left bottom edges to make room for the uprights of a four-poster bed. This treatment is a strong clue that it was a quilt made in New England, borne out by the inscriptions of the quilters, all from central New Hampshire towns.[42] Fisherville was a village north of Concord, New Hampshire's capitol, and is now called Penacook.

Stereograph of Penacook, New Hampshire, ca. 1870. Views of Penacook, once called Fisherville, New Hampshire. *Courtesy of the New Hampshire Historical Society, 07.05.039*

Detail of the Fisherville Friendship Quilt. *Photo by David Bohl*

There is no dedicatory block to explain for whom or why the quilt was made, but the excerpted Bible verses could be taken as advice for a successful marriage. Martha Ordway from Warner, New Hampshire, directs the recipient to "Be faithful until death and ye shall receive a crown of life," a slight rephrasing of a verse from the King James Bible, Revelation 2:10. Mr. and Mrs. G. N. Woodbury of North Weare, New Hampshire, remind the recipient that "Blessed is that household whose God is the Lord." Frank L. Kittredge of Fisherville, New Hampshire, directs the assumed couple to "Be kindly affectioned one toward the other."

YALE ENGINE COMPANY'S QUILT, 1853

Yale Engine Company Quilt, 1853. Unknown makers, South Reading, Massachusetts. Cotton, silk embroidery, 93" by 78". The inscription in the central block states that the quilt is the "Ladies Donation to the Fireman's Fair / Yale Engine Company No. 1 / South Reading / July 1853." *Courtesy of the National Museum of American History; gift of Mrs. Robert Stephens, 1995.001.04*

Firehouse scene showing firemen leaving firehouse pulling a hand-drawn fire engine, ca. 1857. James Fuller Queen, watercolor. The Yale Engine Number 1 looked similar to the fire apparatus depicted here. *Sourced from the Library of Congress, LC-USZC4-6305*

There is a wonderful potholder quilt in the collection of the Smithsonian Institution in Washington, DC, made in South Reading (now Wakefield), Massachusetts, in 1853. As stated on the central block, framed in a floral wreath of cutout appliquéd chintz cotton, it is a fundraising quilt, made to support the Yale Engine Company. The inscription reads: "Ladies' Donation / to the Fireman's Fair / Yale Engine Co. No. 1 / South Reading / July 1853."[51] Whether it was auctioned, raffled, or sold outright, it likely succeeded in raising funds for the cause.

The majority of the quilt's thirty 15½-inch squares were made by folding, cutting the pattern (similar to making folded paper snowflakes), and then appliquéing the cutwork onto the background. It appears that most of the folded patterns have three axis arms, indicating three folds; first in half horizontally, next in half vertically, then quartered on the diagonal. (I will always wonder if the patterns were first cut from paper and used after that step to make the block, or if they were cut directly from folding the fabric.) One block is a pieced star, and another is composed of a pieced American flag with thirteen stars, probably a patriotic nod to the original thirteen states. Two blocks have appliquéd and embroidered circles. One block contains the inscription "Yale Engine Company No. 1, South Reading, 1853" and embroidered depictions of firefighters' equipment, such as a hook, a ladder, and a fire nozzle. The other circle contains an appliquéd and embroidered depiction of the fire engine, again, labeled "York Engine No. 1."

Some of the cutwork blocks are also enhanced by embroidery. Of particular note is a smaller cutwork design near the center of the quilt that uses little of the background real estate of the block and is circled with embroidered leaves and buds. One block has multiple embroidered circles within the cutwork design, and another has four embroidered lyres, one for each corner.

The same red cotton paisley-shaped print is used throughout the quilt with the exception of the flag block, which has carefully cut stripes of a vining motif on a red background. The blocks are layered and quilted, bound with the paisley fabric, and then sewn together.

The inscription states that the quilt was a donation to the Firemen's Fair in July 1853, and there is evidence that there were more fundraising events. An internet search revealed an auction site for the sale of a booklet containing a twelve-page poem written by the Honorable Lilley Eaton, a revered male citizen of the town. The cover states that the poem was delivered at the Firemen's Fair in January 1853, and perhaps copies of the poem were available for sale during or after the event.[52]

William Jeffers manufactured fire engines in Pawtucket, Rhode Island, and was one of several prominent fire apparatus makers in the 1830s and 1840s.[53] The engine purchased from him in 1852 was a hand tub, meant to be drawn and pumped by the volunteers of the fire department. A hand tub engine basically consisted of a wooden water reservoir on wheels, with a pump installed to supply the pressure

Ticket to the Firemen's & Civic Ball, 1858. This ticket for an event in Dover, New Hampshire, is similar to that of a ticket printed for a fundraising event in Wakefield, Massachusetts, to benefit the Yale Engine Company. *Collection of the author*

needed to jet water through hoses. This type of engine was called a hand tub because the reservoir was filled by bucket brigade—lines of people passing empty buckets toward the water supply and sending full ones back to fill the tank on the engine. At least three men lined up on the pump handles, also called brakes, three on each side, to pump the water into the two hoses attached to it, and thus onto the fire. This model also had a suction hose for taking water from a source when it was available close to the fire, and it was able to pump two hose lines at a time.[54]

The fire engine, and the fire company, was named after a major donor to the cause, Burridge Yale. He came to South Reading in 1800 as an itinerant tin peddler and soon established a successful tin-manufacturing business there. Both a history of the town and a history of Middlesex County state that he made a considerable donation toward the purchase of the engine.[55] An astute businessman, he understood the importance of modern fire equipment for the protection of his tin-manufacturing business, which was located across the street from the firehouse, according to a census map from the period.

That first fire station in South Reading was built next to the Town House on Church Street in 1852 at a cost of $970. It was called the Yale No. 1 Station. It burned in 1859 and was replaced with a two-story brick building. The Yale No. 1 engine was saved from this fire, but the two-wheel hose reel was lost. There was another fire-station fire in the 1890s, and the Yale Engine No. 1 was lost.

QUILTS WITH MASONIC SYMBOLS

Presentation quilt with Masonic symbols, 1859. Cotton, wool, 78" by 76". The Masonic symbols include five-pointed stars, the bee skep (hive), and double pillars. *Courtesy of the Washington County Historical Association, Minnesota, 1991.71.02*

Detail of presentation quilt with Masonic symbols

Several potholder quilts display Masonic symbols. Two Civil War quilts (see chapter 5) made by women living on Munjoy Hill, a neighborhood in Portland, Maine, are rich in Freemasonry, or Masonic, symbols, as are two other potholder quilts in this study. One was made in Cumberland County, Maine, and the other was donated to a historical society in Stillwater, Minnesota, dated 1859, with an unknown provenance.

Freemasonry is an international fraternal organization with more than three million members that was formally organized in early-eighteenth-century London. Its purpose is to unite "men of good character who, though of different religious, ethnic, or social backgrounds, share a belief in the fatherhood of God and the brotherhood of mankind."[56] Freemasonry traditions are taught through the allegory of building King Solomon's Temple, and the tools of stonemasons—such as a carpenter's or mason's square and compass—symbolize the lessons of brotherly love, equality, and truth.

Aunt Ada's Quilt, ca. 1850. Probably Cumberland Center, Maine. Cotton, wool, velvet, 88" by 77". The owners found this quilt in an attic in western New Hampshire, but when invited to document it, the author immediately recognized it as a Maine quilt. Many of the signatures are also found on the Cumberland Center Community Church quilts, as are the pieced and appliquéd patterns found in many of the blocks. *Collection of Peter Bixby and Francelle Carapetyan*

Oak Leaf and Reel Quilt, ca. 1850. Susan Batchelder, Bath, Maine. Cotton, 75" by 65". The oak leaf and reel pattern is found in many potholder blocks in this period. Sadly, the quilt has been washed, and only the name "Susan Batchelder" remains legible. The blocks were signed on the back. *Maine State Museum, Augusta, Maine. 2011.29.1; photo by David Bohl*

Detail of the Oak Leaf and Reel Quilt. Maine State Museum, Augusta, Maine. 2011.29.1. *Photo by David Bohl*

CHAPTER 5

THE AMERICAN CIVIL WAR 1861–1865

The popularity of potholder quilts during the mid-nineteenth century spanned the years of the American Civil War, 1861–1865.

Note: Civil War quilts are covered in great detail in the author's book on the subject. This short chapter gives a brief overview of quilting for the Civil War cause and details one quilt.

When the war broke out, the armies were unprepared to supply the needs of their soldiers. Women, both in the North and the South, formed new soldiers' aid societies or reorganized existing ones to provide bedding, clothing, food, and medical supplies. Clothing and bedding were most requested, and women made new quilts and donated existing bedcovers.[59]

In the North, the United States Sanitary Commission (USSC) was created to improve conditions for soldiers on the battlefield and in camps, hospitals, and prisons. The USSC solicited aid from the home front, coordinated the relief efforts of local groups, and channeled donated supplies to the areas of greatest need. There were many other aid societies, including the Christian Commission,[60] and several states formally organized aid for their own boys in camps and hospitals. The Sanitary Commission published bulletins listing needed items, specifying "quilts of cheap materials, four feet wide by 84 inches long."[61]

Northern women donated an estimated 250,000 quilts during the war years, perhaps half of these through the USSC and the rest through local and state organizations.[62] While the total number of quilts made or donated on both sides will never be known, only about twenty quilts made for Civil War soldiers are known to exist. All the survivors are inscribed quilts, and eleven of these are potholder quilts. Of further significance, all but two of these potholder quilts made for Civil War soldiers originated either in Maine or Massachusetts. One of the two exceptions was made in Granville, New York, a town that sits on the Vermont border. The Detroit, Michigan, quilt includes signatures and place names; of the eighty-two named places, twelve are in Massachusetts or New Hampshire. Of these eleven potholder quilts, only four display the stamp of the Sanitary Commission, but eight others are long and narrow, as specified in commission bulletins.

In addition to specifying the size for donated quilts,

Detail of the Portland Album Quilt (page 90). Several of the Civil War album quilts have patriotic symbols like the Union Shield seen here. *Collection of the Maine State Museum, Augusta, Maine, 2015.11.1; photo courtesy of James D. Julia, Inc.*

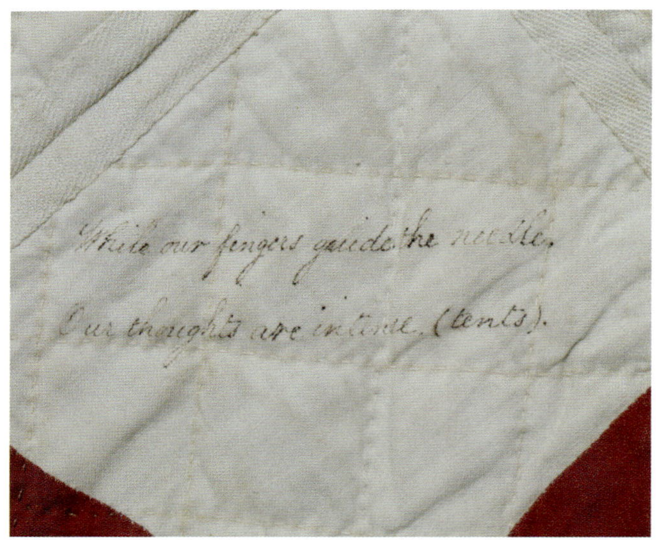

Detail of the Portland Album Quilt (page 90). The inscription reads: "While our fingers guide the needle, Our thoughts are intense (tents)." *Photo by Mike Taylor*

Illustration from *The Tribute Book*, 1865. This book by Frank B. Goodrich is a record of the work done by those serving on the home front during the Civil War, with emphasis on women's work, and is filled with illustrations such as this. *Collection of the author*

one bulletin suggested writing on the quilts and adding signatures.[63] Ten of the Civil War potholder quilts exhibit multiple inscriptions, reflecting various sentiments meant to entertain, enlighten, amuse, and encourage soldiers. The inscriptions include patriotic slogans, health tips, Bible verses, and puns. Some contain excerpted lines from poetry and hymns, invectives against strong drink or tobacco use, and riddles.[64] The wide range of inscriptions and variations in penmanship indicates the work of many hands.

Of the eleven Civil War potholder quilts, six feature repeating block patterns, and five are variety quilts. Among these quilts, block sizes range from 7½ inches square in a quilt with ninety-three blocks, to 16 inches square in a quilt with twenty blocks. Three of the quilts contain a larger central block containing either a Union shield or a flag. The makers of a fourth quilt achieved a central focus with the placement of nine blocks containing red, white, and blue fabrics. All but two of the quilts employ a wide range of scrap fabrics in the piecing or appliqué.

Three of the Civil War potholder quilts include one or more blocks that are machine-quilted, and at least one also contains machine piecing and machine appliqué. Sewing machines became commercially available during the decade before the war, and women who owned them put them to use in their relief efforts.

All the Civil War potholder quilts are inscribed with dates. The earliest was completed in August 1863, and the latest in February 1865. Three quilts are inscribed both with start and finish dates, which indicate that one quilt took a few weeks to complete, a second six months, and the third a full year. I suspect that the makers of the quilts taking the longest time collected these blocks as they could and perhaps made other quilts in that time.

The Civil War potholder quilts served not only to comfort the soldiers but to raise money for relief efforts. Seven of the Civil War potholder quilts were made long and narrow as recommended by the Sanitary Commission bulletin, suggesting that they were made for soldiers' use in the field or a hospital. These quilts were intended to provide not simply physical comfort, but mental, emotional, and spiritual solace as well. Ten of the eleven are inscribed with names, place names, poetry, and Bible verses, while the remaining one is inscribed only with names and place names. The fabrics are drawn from a wide selection of dressmaking and decorator fabrics available before the war.

Detail of the Portland Album Quilt (page 90). Many of the blocks in this quilt are heavily inscribed. *Photo by Mike Taylor*

PORTLAND ALBUM QUILT

Portland Album Quilt, 1864. Attributed to Carrie Davis and Cornelia Dow, Portland, Maine. Cotton, 81" by 71". The majority of the inscriptions in the quilt's central area are those of Carrie Davis and Cornelia M. Dow. There are also several names inscribed that include a town of origin and "Home Institute." *Photo by Mike Taylor*

A Civil War soldiers' quilt dated 1864 and made in Portland, Maine, is patriotic in the use of the Union shield in its center medallion, which is surrounded by blocks appliquéd with red or blue five-pointed stars. Each of the blocks contains four or five inscriptions that are patriotic or religious in nature, and many also contain temperance slogans and messages. Research into the signers of the blocks revealed stories about the role that Maine's educated women played in advocating for social change and as leaders in education.

This quilt was most likely made as a fundraiser or for display, since it exceeds the recommended width of 48 inches (to fit a cot or hospital bed) by more than 20 inches. It contains sixty-eight 9-inch-square star blocks alternating in red and blue solid fabrics, each bound with off-white woven cotton tape and whipstitched together. The center is an 18-inch square with a pieced and appliquéd Union shield, embroidered with stars and displaying many inscriptions, including a drawing of an eagle. That central medallion includes the names Cornelia A. Dow and Carrie E. Davis, and their names are found on eight and nine other blocks, respectively, leading to the conclusion that they were the project organizers.[65]

Carrie Davis was the daughter of Caroline Eliza Thorndike Davis and Woodbury Davis, who was a Maine Supreme Court judge at this time and later became the postmaster of Portland. He was involved both in the antislavery and temperance movements.[66] Carrie was nineteen years old when the quilt was made. The 1860 and 1870 censuses list the family of three members, with the confusing addition of Carrie's name now listed as Caroline. There are blocks signed by Caroline Davis, so perhaps Carrie's mother also made some blocks. Cornelia Dow and Carrie Davis were neighbors, with the Dows living at 714 Congress Street and the Davis family at 727 Congress Street.

Cornelia Maria Dow was the daughter of Maria Cornelia Durant Maynard Dow. Her father, Neal Dow, was a national leader in the temperance movement, a former mayor of Portland, and a Civil War brigadier general commanding the 13th Maine Infantry. Dow was wounded in one of the battles of the siege of Vicksburg, and on June 30, 1862, while recovering, he was captured by a Confederate cavalry unit and eventually imprisoned in Richmond, Virginia, at Libby Prison. In February 1864, he was exchanged for General Robert E. Lee's son, William Henry Lee, and returned to Portland, where he resigned from the army in November 1864.[67]

Cornelia was also active in temperance work at the national level, serving on local, state, and national committees for the Women's Christian Temperance Union (WCTU), where she was appointed treasurer of the trust fund used to retire the debt of the Chicago branch of the organization in 1898.[68] She died in October 1905, and an essay expressing appreciation for her lifelong work appeared in the 1906 report of the Maine WCTU bulletin, stating that for the promotion of temperance she "gave her time, her influence and her money. . . . She had the love and confidence of Frances E. Willard (national president)[,] who selected her for a most important charge in connection with our work."

Louise Hammond and her sister Julia D. Hammond, who married Cornelia's brother Frederick Neal Dow in October 1864, signed the quilt, as did Mary Springer, listing her home as Matazas, Cuba. Emily P. Woodward and Helen D. Chapman signed their names followed by "Home Institute," as did Isabella Prince. Research revealed that many of the young women who inscribed their names and home cities far from Portland were being educated at the Home Institute on Free Street in Portland.

The principal of the Home Institute was Isabella Graham Prince, and head teacher was her sister, Mary Gray Prince. The Yarmouth (Maine) Historical Society holds correspondence and many undated newspaper clippings about these remarkable women.[69] Both graduated from the North Yarmouth Academy in Yarmouth, Maine, and one undated and unsourced newspaper clipping states that "Capt. and Mrs. Prince were most ambitious for their daughters and it was their aim to give them as good advantages as though 'they had been boys.'" Their father was a ship's master, and the newspaper accounts indicate that both girls traveled with their father on his voyages to Europe and received advanced education in languages in New York City. Both women taught all their lives and founded their own schools.

There is only one bulletin advertising the Home Institute at the Maine Historical Society in Portland, and it is dated 1859–60. It lists thirteen boarding students from towns as far away as Vicksburg, Mississippi, and St. John, New Brunswick, and eleven local day pupils are registered. Quoting from the bulletin: "It is the aim of the Teachers of the Home Institute to educate

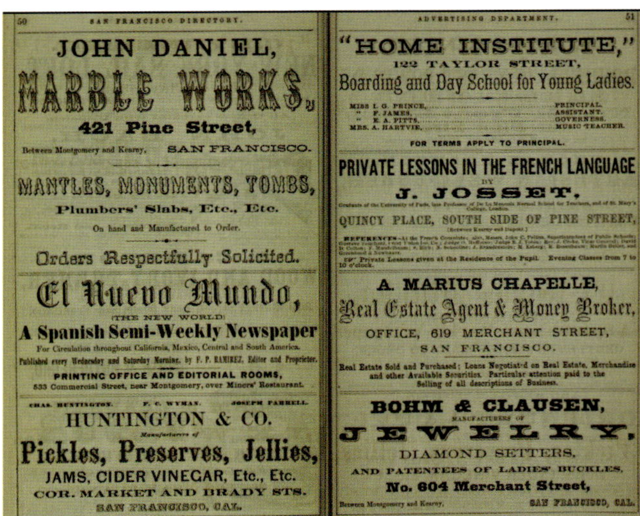
50 SAN FRANCISCO DIRECTORY.

JOHN DANIEL,
MARBLE WORKS,
421 Pine Street,
Between Montgomery and Kearny, SAN FRANCISCO.
MANTLES, MONUMENTS, TOMBS,
Plumbers' Slabs, Etc., Etc.
On hand and Manufactured to Order.
Orders Respectfully Solicited.

El Nuevo Mundo,
(THE NEW WORLD)
A Spanish Semi-Weekly Newspaper
For Circulation throughout California, Mexico, Central and South America.
Published every Wednesday and Saturday Morning, by F. P. RAMIREZ, Editor and Proprietor.
PRINTING OFFICE AND EDITORIAL ROOMS,
533 Commercial Street, near Montgomery, over Miners' Restaurant.

CHAS. HUNTINGTON. F. C. WYMAN. JOSEPH FARRELL.
HUNTINGTON & CO.
Manufacturers of
Pickles, Preserves, Jellies,
JAMS, CIDER VINEGAR, Etc., Etc.
COR. MARKET AND BRADY STS.
SAN FRANCISCO, CAL.

ADVERTISING DEPARTMENT. 51

"HOME INSTITUTE,"
122 TAYLOR STREET,
Boarding and Day School for Young Ladies.
MISS I. G. PRINCE, ... PRINCIPAL.
" F. JAMES, ... ASSISTANT.
" E. A. PITTS, ... GOVERNESS.
MRS. A. HARTVIE, ... MUSIC TEACHER.
FOR TERMS APPLY TO PRINCIPAL.

PRIVATE LESSONS IN THE FRENCH LANGUAGE
BY
J. JOSSET,
QUINCY PLACE, SOUTH SIDE OF PINE STREET,
Private Lessons given at the Residence of the Pupil. Evening Classes from 7 to 10 o'clock.

A. MARIUS CHAPELLE,
Real Estate Agent & Money Broker,
OFFICE, 619 MERCHANT STREET,
SAN FRANCISCO.
Real Estate Sold and Purchased; Loans Negotiated on Real Estate, Merchandise and other Available Securities. Particular attention paid to the Selling of all descriptions of Business.

BOHM & CLAUSEN,
MANUFACTURERS OF
JEWELRY,
DIAMOND SETTERS,
AND PATENTEES OF LADIES' BUCKLES,
No. 604 Merchant Street,
Between Montgomery and Kearny, SAN FRANCISCO, CAL.

An advertisement for the Home Institute was sourced online from the 1878 San Francisco city directory.

Mary G. Prince, ca. 1880, Yokohama, Japan. The formal portrait records the name of the photographer in Yokohama, where Mary and her sister were administrators and instructors in an American-run high school. *Courtesy of the Yarmouth, Maine, Historical Society*

the young ladies entrusted to their care, in all that pertains to the character of 'a perfect woman nobly planned,' and as brilliancy of intellect is frequently obscured by want of cultivation in manner, no pains will be spared to inspire a due regard for propriety and elegance." Studies included French, music, and drawing and painting, and attention was given to recreation "as part of a regimine [*sic*] conducive to the general improvement of mind and body."

The Home Institute and its principals disappear from the Portland city directory after the war, but their trail leads to San Francisco. The 1867 San Francisco city directory contains an advertisement for a Home Institute with "Isabella G. Prince" as resident principal. The school advertises as a boarding and day school for young ladies, offering music, languages, mathematics, and calisthenics.[70] The State of California Department of Education requires annual reports, and in the 1876 directory of schools, Isabella writes to explain her school:

> The Home Institute, a boarding and day school for young ladies[, is] under the supervision of Miss Isabella G. Prince. . . . It may be considered as a permanent institution, as the property was purchased and building erected expressly for school purposes. It is intended to be what its name indicates, a *home school*, where the advantages of careful instruction in the various branches of a solid education are combined with every home pleasure and necessary accomplishment. . . . It . . . was established, has been controlled, and instructed by its present Principal.[71]

Isabella G. Prince, ca. 1880, Yokohama, Japan. *Courtesy of the Yarmouth, Maine, Historical Society*

Mary Prince eventually joined her sister to teach in San Francisco. A newspaper article written at the time of Mary Prince's death reports that both women administered and taught in San Francisco for several years and then were invited to teach at a high school in Japan. The article explains that several young Japanese women attended the Home Institute, and the Japanese government thought it important to establish "American" schools for girls.[72]

Several more undated newspaper articles from the period illuminate their travel and teaching and their return to Yarmouth in 1906.[73] They lived with cousins in Portland until they died—Isabella in 1912 and Mary in 1918—and were active in the area, delivering many lectures on the culture and history of Japan.

GALLERY OF QUILTS

Album Quilt, 1864. Made by the Fort Hill Ladies Sewing Circle, Hingham, Massachusetts. Cotton, 83" by 53½". The Fort Hill Ladies Sewing Circle was originally organized in the 1850s to raise money to restore the ancient Fort Hill Cemetery in Hingham. The author found evidence of the continuation of the group into the 1920s. *Courtesy of the International Quilt Museum, University of Nebraska–Lincoln, 2013.609.8*

Album Quilt, 1864. Attributed to Charlotte F. Hussey with various signers, Detroit, Michigan. Cotton, 93" by 58". Although it was made in Detroit, many signatures were gathered from New England, and Charlotte Hussey was from Massachusetts. *Courtesy of the International Quilt Museum, University of Nebraska–Lincoln, 1997.007.0569*

Album Quilt, 1863. Organized by Susannah G. Pullen with her Sunday School Scholars, Augusta, Maine. Cotton, 84" by 50". The fifteen blocks are finished knife edge and inscribed with puns, riddles, Bible verses, and health advice. *National Museum of American History; gift of Mrs. Charlotte Pullen Scruton, T.7726*

Pieced Album Quilt, ca. 1865. Various makers, Granville, New York. Cotton, 79" by 56". Note the block in the center depicting the US flag. *Courtesy of the Wadsworth Atheneum Museum of Art, Hartford, Connecticut; gift of Mrs. Emerson C. Taylor, 1929.212; photo by Allen Phillips*

Album Quilt, 1865. Attributed to Susan Loring Jackson, Beverly Farms, Massachusetts. Cotton, 84" by 56". Susan L. Jackson signed several of the blocks as well as the names of her two youngest children. Both her eldest son, Patrick Tracy Jackson, and her brother, Charles Greely Loring, served in the Union army. *Collection of the Rochester Historical Association, Rochester, New York, 2004.511; photo by David Bohl*

Album Quilt, 1864. Made by the Ladies Aid Society of Portland, Maine. Cotton, silk, 80½" by 58½". The Munjoy Hill Civil War quilts were made in the neighborhood in Portland, Maine, that surrounds the Portland Observatory. Both quilts have several blocks made by the same women, including depictions of the observatory. *Collection of the Mystic Seaport Museum, Mystic, Connecticut, 1968.24*

Album Quilt, 1864. Made by the Ladies Aid Society of Portland, Maine. Cotton, silk, 86½" by 68½". This quilt and the related quilt each have anchors, the symbol of hope; eagles; and a double-ended steamship sitting on a ribbon of silk. Masonic symbols are also included. *Courtesy of the Brickstore Museum, Kennebunk, Maine, 2453; photo by C. A. Smith*

Album Quilt, 1865. Attributed to Rebecca B. Sibley, Boston, Massachusetts. Cotton, 87½" by 58½". James George of the 76th Regiment of the New York Infantry was the recipient of this quilt, probably when admitted to a hospital in Washington, DC. He fought in the Battles of Gettysburg and Fredericksburg but was captured and imprisoned in Andersonville, Georgia, and released in February 1865. *Courtesy of the New England Quilt Museum, Lowell, Massachusetts, 2004.17; photo by David Stansbury*

Reverse of the Album Quilt attributed to Rebecca B. Sibley. *Photo by David Stansbury*

Album Quilt, 1863. Unknown makers, Norrigewock, Maine. Cotton, 84" by 63". Laura Syler appraised this quilt in Texas in the early 1990s but lost contact with the owners, and the quilt's location is unknown. *Private collection; photo by Laura Syler*

Album Quilt, 1863. Attributed to the Ladies' Industrial Union, Florence, Massachusetts. Cotton, 85" by 53". The Free Congregational Society of Florence published a report in which the author found several of the names on the quilt that could be puzzled out from the photographs. The Ladies Industrial Union was organized to "do good works." *Private collection; photo courtesy of American Hurrah archives*

Crosses and Losses Quilt, 1864. Various makers, Saco, Maine. Cotton, 70" by 69". Historian Stephanie Hatch believes this quilt was made for donation to the Civil War cause, due to the red, white, and blue colors. *Collection of the author; photo by David Bohl*

CHAPTER 6

A MULTITUDE OF FABRICS 1866–1900

CAPTAIN MUSAUS QUILT, 1867

Captain Musaus Quilt, 1867. Various signers, probably organized by Henrietta Purinton Musaus, Portland, Maine. Cotton, 89" by 70". The quilt was probably made to celebrate the retirement or sale of Captain Charles Musaus's interest in this ship. It is covered with nautical objects and ship's pennants and flags and is inscribed by the family and friends of Captain Musaus and his wife. *From* Antiques Roadshow, *#1802, Boise, Hour 2, ©1997–2019 WGBH; photo by Jeff Dunn for WGBH, ©WGBH 2019; collection of the Maine State Museum, Augusta, Maine, 2020.1.1*

My phone started ringing around 8 p.m. on a Monday night in December 2013. Excited friends were watching the Boise, Idaho, episode of *Antiques Roadshow* and spotted a textile that was obviously a potholder quilt. The stitching along the bottom row of blocks had let go, leaving three blocks hanging. I tuned in to hear Stephen Fletcher, an appraiser from Skinner, in Boston, interviewing the owner, who is a great-great granddaughter of Captain Charles Frederick Musaus, the Portland, Maine, sea captain for whom family tradition said the quilt was made.[74]

I contacted WGBH, the Boston television company that produces *Road Show*, and asked that the quilt owners contact me, which they did. In August 2014, I traveled to Sacramento, California, and met the quilt and its owners. I transcribed the names, examined the motifs on the quilt, and learned of its travels.

Most of the sixty-three blocks have red motifs appliquéd to a white background, several are pieced, and all are machine-quilted. Two double-sized blocks contain the US and Norwegian flags. There is a ship's pennant with the name *Norwegian*; depictions of navigation tools, Masonic symbols, and a Union shield; and an appliquéd and embroidered block depicting the Portland Observatory. Four other quilts made in Cumberland County, Maine, have similar blocks featuring the observatory, the appliquéd eagle, a fouled anchor (symbol of hope), and tools for navigation. The block makers and signers include Captain Musaus's wife, Marrietta Gould Purinton Musaus, and her mother, sisters, aunts, cousins, and neighbors. Several women made and signed multiple blocks.[75]

An entry in the *American Lloyd's Registry of American and Foreign Shipping* in 1864 lists Musaus as captain of the *Norwegian*, an 887-ton bark (which is generally defined as a ship rigged with three masts) registered to Briggs and Cushing, shipbuilders in Freeport, Maine. The quilt is dated August 11, 1867. The *American Neptune, a Quarterly Journal of Maritime History*, reports that the *Norwegian* was sold in 1867 to a British company, HWMV of Hamilton, Bermuda. Perhaps Captain Musaus owned shares in the company and benefited from the sale, and perhaps the quilt was made to commemorate Captain Musaus's retirement from service as the ship's captain. The entry also states that in 1881 the *Norwegian* was reported missing en route from New York to Liverpool with a cargo of petroleum.

Captain Charles Frederick Musaus emigrated from Norway to Maine as a young teenager and became a United States citizen in 1854.[76] Through census records, Portland museum records of donations, and newspaper accounts, I pieced together bits of his interesting life. Musaus is listed as a master mariner in the US census from the 1850s to the 1880s.

He was married twice, and it was his second wife, Marietta Gould Purinton, twenty-eight years his junior, or her younger sister Harriet, who probably organized the making of the quilt to celebrate either the sale or

Holly Matthews and Susan Awalt are sisters and great-granddaughters of Captain Charles Musaus.

Detail of the Captain Musaus Quilt. A carefully embroidered pennant with the name of the ship.

Detail of the Captain Musaus Quilt. The Portland Observatory stands on Munjoy Hill in Portland, Maine. Five Cumberland County, Maine, quilts have blocks with various depictions of this landmark.

Detail of the Captain Musaus Quilt. A block bearing a nautical compass. The makers' names are inscribed on the back of each block.

Correspondence to and from Captain Musaus was passed down through three generations with the quilt.

his captaincy of the *Norwegian*. Marietta accompanied him on several voyages, and one of their sons was born at sea. Marietta died in 1878 at age thirty-eight. Captain Musaus died in Liverpool, England, where he is on the voter registration lists and in the census as a corn merchant, and where the notice of his death and probate appear in 1888. His younger son, Charles, was an executor and traveled to Liverpool to settle the estate. Captain Musaus and both wives are buried in the Evergreen Cemetery in Portland, Maine.

Susan Musaus Matthews was the youngest daughter of Marietta and Charles Musaus. The quilt descended in the Matthews family and in 2020 was donated to the Maine State Museum.

These two quilts beg so many questions. Did a pattern or a suggestion for such unusual construction appear somewhere in print? Did the maker of the *Pieced Explosion* quilt know the maker of the *Compass* quilt and vow to do a more complicated and better-executed version? Or did the maker of the *Compass* see the *Pieced Explosion* and say, "I can make that!" (and then couldn't)?

Compass Quilt, ca. 1870. Unknown maker, Pennsylvania. Cotton, 86" by 65". The quilt's larger blocks set in a dark background make a stunning statement. *Collection of the International Quilt Museum, University of Nebraska–Lincoln, 1997.007.0949*

Detail of the back of the Compass Quilt, showing an intersection of a round block and two setting pieces

Detail of the Compass Quilt. The maker had difficulty fitting the block into its space in the quilt.

Detail of the top of the Compass Quilt, showing the intersection of a round block and two setting pieces

TWO ENGLISH QUILTS

A most unusual way to make quilts block by block appears in two English quilts in the study. The blocks are composed of a plain muslin backing and a muslin top block that is slightly smaller. The top is decorated with applied shapes and sometimes strips of fabric; it is similar in appearance to tile quilts. The top block is stitched to the backing block, with no batting in between. A small border of the backing block shows around the edges of the top block, forming a thin frame, which is characteristic of this technique.

The collectors who own these quilts purchased them at different times from the same dealer, who purchased them in England. The quilt owned by Lisa Erlandson has multiple Bible verses inscribed and is similar to scripture quilts seen in British quilt history books.[81] Carol Gebel's quilt does not have inscriptions, but both quilts seem to share the same color and arrangement sensibility.

Medallion Quilt, ca. 1880. Unknown maker, England. Cotton, 95" by 74". The backing of each block is brought to the front and folded over, then strips are appliquéd on top to create each block. *Collection of Carol Gebel; photo by David Bohl*

English Medallion Quilt, ca. 1880. Unknown maker, England. Cotton, 80" by 73". This medallion quilt is inscribed with biblical scripture in the center block. *Collection of Lisa Erlandson; photo by David Bohl*

Detail of the Medallion Quilt. Note the similarity to tile quilts, where fabrics are applied on the surface of the blocks. *Photo by David Bohl*

Detail of the English Medallion Quilt. *Photo by David Bohl*

BRUBAKER ALBUM QUILT, 1872

A member of the Potholder Posse alerted me to a quilt in the collection of the Brethren Heritage Center in Brookville, Ohio. In 2009, I stopped at this museum and resource center to see the quilt and interview Gale Honeyman, who was then the curator of the collection of objects relating to the Brethren. The Brethren are a religious group similar to the Mennonites; they generally include seven distinct groups of Protestant sects descending from a group of Anabaptists who first organized in Germany in 1707 and eventually immigrated to the American colonies to escape persecution.[82] Honeyman described them as being a "plain people, dressing in dark colors, never red." When I asked specifically about women's dress fabrics, he explained that at one time there was a proscribed pattern for women's clothing and that the women's dresses could more recently be made of prints with very small patterns.[83]

Brubaker Album Quilt, 1872. Made by the friends and family of James A. Brubaker, Bedford County, Virginia. Wool, cotton, silk, 87" by 68". Scarlet tanagers, flowers, and baskets pieced in bright primary and secondary colors grace this cheerful quilt. Many of the inscriptions are just initials, but enough full names are included to identify Brubaker relations. *Collection of the Brethren Heritage Center, Brookville, Ohio; gift of Carolyn Miller Davalunas; photo by David Bohl*

The Brethren quilt was made for James A. Brubaker as a bachelor's quilt, according to Mr. Honeyman, and is dated 1872. James Brubaker left his home in Virginia sometime in his midtwenties and walked great distances, visiting and staying extended periods with family members along the way. He traveled by foot from Otter Township in Bedford County, Virginia, to Iowa, back through Illinois, and eventually to Ohio, where he settled with a cousin and met his future wife. In 1876, he married Elizabeth C. Arnold, also of Virginia. Honeyman explained that it was common for some members of Brethren sects to take walking trips between relatives, helping on their farms, visiting distant cousins, and often finding a bride.

The sixty-three 10-inch blocks are made mostly of wools, with some cottons (with tiny prints) and silks, and are constructed with piecing, appliqué, and embroidery. The batting is very light and the quilting is sparse. More than half the blocks have signatures or initials. Some are members of Brubaker's family, including his sisters, named Adria, Calpirnia, and Sarah Jane. Varner family members were from the nearby village of Liberty in Bedford County; Mary E. Varner and her daughter Florida M. signed as well. Although there are forty blocks with some kind of inscription, the majority of blocks have initials only, and it is not

Log Cabin with Stripes, ca. 1890. Unknown maker. Cotton. The woman who designed this quilt was a genius; she carefully cut across the red-and navy-blue-striped fabric so that the dark-value logs appear as tiny blue and red squares. Each block is bound in such a way that there is no interruption of the overall pattern. *Collection of the author*

Detail of the Log Cabin with Stripes. All the blocks are individually bound, but the maker chose to put a red binding around the outer edge of the quilt.

ADMISSION DAY QUILT, 1890

Admission Day Crazy Quilt, ca. 1890. Unknown maker, California. Silk, ribbons, 64" by 58". Each block is 5", elegantly pieced, embroidered, or painted pillow. *Collection of the author; photo by David Bohl*

Detail of the Bradford Grand Army of the Republic Quilt. This block has more information about one person than any other on the quilt, including the officers of Post 58.

Detail of the Bradford Grand Army of the Republic Quilt. GAR Post 58 was named to honor a Sutton, New Hampshire, soldier who died in Virginia in a skirmish in 1863. Membership in this post was open to several towns, including Bradford. *Collection of the Bradford (NH) Historical Society*

Benjamin F. Stephenson founded the Grand Army of the Republic in Decatur, Illinois, in 1866. "The membership was limited to honorably discharged veterans of the Union Army, Navy, Marine Corps, or Revenue Cutter Service who had served between April 12, 1861[,] and April 9, 1865." Originally founded with the intention to unite veterans for fraternal and social activities, the GAR quickly evolved into an organization that fought for better veterans' benefits and supported political candidates. It founded veterans' homes and lobbied for better medical care and pensions.[92] The GAR groups were active in New Hampshire and elsewhere, holding reunions on the local and state levels, with members attending regional and even national gatherings.

The membership in each state was organized as a "department," and each department had multiple "posts," numbered in order of their founding. Each post had a name as well as a number; the posts were named for a service person who was dead. GAR Post #58 (inscribed on the quilt) included veterans from several towns, including Bradford, and was named for Lieutenant Robert M. Campbell, resident of nearby Sutton, New Hampshire, who served in the First New England Cavalry for three years. He rose from private to lieutenant and in June 1863 was killed in a skirmish while commanding a picket line on an outpost in White Oak Swamp, Virginia. His body was not recovered.[93]

Dr. Cyrus M. Fisk's name appears among the thirty other inscriptions on the quilt, and his contains more information than any other block. While in his late teens, he apprenticed with a physician in central New Hampshire and then took his medical degree from Dartmouth College in 1847. He began his medical practice in Bradford in 1848 and remained there for twenty-four years, interrupted by his Civil War service. Fisk was appointed assistant surgeon and served with the Sixteenth Regiment New Hampshire Volunteers from November 1862 to August 1863, when he was discharged with his regiment and ranked deputy surgeon. In 1872, he joined a partnership in Lowell, Massachusetts, where he practiced medicine, was a member of several medical organizations, and was an advisory physician of the Lowell General Hospital. He retired back to Bradford in 1894 and died there the

Left to right: Women's Relief Fund lapel pin, GAR Memorial Day postcard, and a GAR lapel pin, all ca. 1900. The Grand Army of the Republic was credited with the creation of Memorial Day. The lapel pins were worn at reunions. *Collection of the author*

following year. The history of the Sixteenth Regiment states that while living in Lowell, Dr. Fisk was active in the Ladd and Whitney Post #185, Department of Massachusetts GAR. Because his name appears on the Bradford quilt, I assume that he joined G.A.R. Post 58 upon his retirement to Bradford in the early 1890s, which coincides with the probable date of the quilt, circa 1890.[94]

One of the other potholder quilts in the Bradford Historical Society's collection is also made of shoofly blocks. Instead of using just two fabrics (like the GAR quilt), it contains a wonderful variety of dark cotton calicos dating from the 1870s and 1880s, and the quilt contains the date 1889. It is machine pieced and quilted, and the white binding on several of the blocks is applied by machine. The blocks are individually signed or have stamped or stenciled names, and more than one has penmanship similar to that seen on the GAR quilt.

The third Bradford potholder quilt is a fundraising quilt worked in another style popular in the last quarter of the nineteenth century—redwork embroidery. Redwork quilts are made by embroidering blocks of light-colored fabric, often muslin or other medium-weight cotton, with outlined figures of people, animals, flowers, and even popular cartoons in red cotton stitch. Patterns could be traced from women's magazines, purchased from the local dry-goods store, or ordered as iron transfer patterns from newspapers. Of course, embroiderers could even make up their own. Block sizes range from 4 to 5 inches up to 20 inches. The smaller blocks contain one motif, and larger blocks may contain one or many motifs.

The Bradford quilt's history was recorded by one of the women involved in the project, and her typed note is still attached to it:

Dr. Cyrus Fisk, ca. 1880. Dr. Fisk served with the 16th Regiment of New Hampshire Volunteers as deputy surgeon. After the war he practiced medicine in Lowell, Massachusetts, for twenty years and returned to Bradford in his retirement. *Courtesy of the Saint Anselm College Library*

> The Ladies' Aid Society of the First Baptist Church of Bradford made this quilt to raise money for the remodeling of the church vestry. Each block has one person's name prominently embroidered in its center. This person (nearly all women) paid one dollar for the square, and in turn secured a dime from [each of the] many other people who signed her square. The quilt was then auctioned in the Town Hall in the late 1890s (the quilt is dated 1896) and purchased by Mr. George Brown, a prominent Concord, NH, businessman who resided in Bradford. In 1953, the quilt was donated to the Women's Christian Guild by Mrs. Gladys Emmerson MacPhee of Andover, NH. No one is certain as to how the quilt came into her possession.[95]

Every block on the quilt shares the same pattern of a ribbonlike cartouche that scrolls diagonally across the quilt block, with the block organizer's name embroidered there. Surrounding this are thirty to forty more embroidered names. There are men, women, couples, children, and even the name of someone's cat. This quilt is a great example of the many fundraising quilts made between 1880 and 1920, often red and white, and always with hundreds of names inked or embroidered.

Detail of the Bradford Friendship Quilt, 1889. Unknown maker, Bradford, New Hampshire. Cotton. The handwriting on this block is the same as is found on every block on the Bradford G.A.R. quilt. Was Elva J. Bailey the organizer of both quilts? *Collection of the Bradford (NH) Historical Society*

Detail of the Bradford Redwork Fundraising Quilt. Unknown maker, Bradford, New Hampshire. Cotton. *Collection of the Bradford (NH) Historical Society*

GALLERY OF QUILTS

Potholder-Style Sampler Quilt, ca. 1885. Unknown maker. Cotton, 88¾" by 76". The 120 7½" blocks are bound in tan or red cotton. *Collection of Lynn Miller; photo by Lynne Miller*

Detail of the Potholder-Style Sampler Quilt. The seams between the bound blocks are embellished with a herringbone embroidery stitch, and each corner is decorated with a crocheted flower. *Collection of Lynn Miller; photo by Lynne Miller*

Crosses and Losses Quilt, ca. 1900. Unknown maker, collected in Maine. Cotton, 74" by 74". A simple repeated pattern can make a strong impression. *Collection of the author; photo by David Bohl*

LeMoyne Star, ca. 1880. Unknown maker, probably Pennsylvania. Cotton, 66" by 66". This remarkable quilt was made by someone who loved her sewing machine. The blocks are pieced, quilted, and bound by machine, and the leaf motifs are machine-appliquéd. *Collection of the International Quilt Museum, University of Nebraska–Lincoln, 2006.043.0087*

Emery Presentation Quilt, 1878. Various makers, Littleton, New Hampshire. Cotton and wool, 87" by 79". Probably made for the Reverend Ira Emery, pastor of the Free Will Baptist Church. *Collection of the author; photo by David Bohl*

CHAPTER 7

FUNDRAISING AND FOLDED QUILTS 1901–1969

FUNDRAISING QUILTS

The styles seen in twentieth-century quilt as you go quilts mirror the general fads of each period. Several potholder fundraising quilts made between 1890 and 1930 feature redwork embroidery, hundreds of signatures, and blocks bound in red cotton. The Ladies Aid and Missionary Society of the Union Congregational Church of Madbury, New Hampshire, started a fundraising quilt in 1914 and completed it in the early 1930s, according to records kept with the quilt.[96] A donation of ten cents was collected for each name, and more than $75 was raised for the society's charitable works.

The fifty-six 11-inch-square blocks each contain an embroidered 9-inch circle divided like a pie into twelve pieces. Each "pie slice" is embroidered with many names, and some of the squares were embroidered by the family or group who committed the funds. On some of the blocks, these groups or makers initialed or signed their blocks with the names of individuals, social clubs, or other service groups in the town. Lorie Chase, who brought the quilt to my attention, counted more than 1,100 names on the quilt.

Seven hundred seventy-seven names are inked on the backs of the forty-nine machine-quilted potholder blocks in a red-and-white monkey wrench quilt made in West Concord, Vermont.[97] The center block is inscribed with the name of the group, "The YPCU of West Concord, Vermont, 1895," which is the Young People's Christian Union, affiliated with the Universalist Church. The quilt is in the collection of the Concord (Vermont) Historical Society, and the society believes that each person whose name appears on the quilt donated to the project.

From what can be seen of the quilt blocks in the book *Plain and Fancy*, it appears that family groups or individuals took responsibility for a block. Some are simply covered in names, while others appear sparse, and the handwriting is not uniform. West Concord was one of five villages now incorporated into the town of Concord.[98] The town's population reached its peak in 1880 with 1,660 residents, so nearly half of them participated in this fundraiser.

Ladies Aid Fundraising Quilt, ca. 1915. Ladies Aid and Missionary Society of the Union Congregational Church, Madbury, New Hampshire. Cotton, 92" by 81". There are 1,100 names embroidered on this quilt, which raised $75 for the society and is a record of other groups active in the town at the time. *Collection of the Madbury (NH) Historical Society*

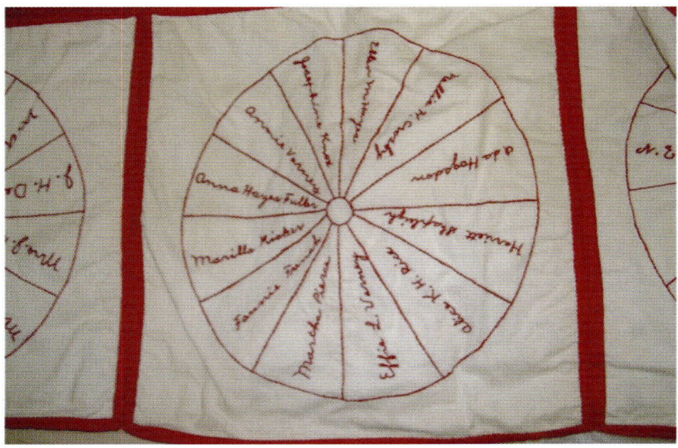

Detail of the embroidered wheel pattern on the Ladies Aid Fundraising Quilt. *Collection of the Madbury (NH) Historical Society*

VARIETY QUILTS

Album Quilt, ca. 1910. Unknown maker. Cotton, 77½" by 66". The forty-two 10" blocks are a wonderful assortment of patterns popular in the late nineteenth century. *Collection of the International Quilt Museum, University of Nebraska–Lincoln, 2008.040.0092*

Album Quilt, ca. 1920. Unknown maker. Cotton, 64" by 63". Most of the blocks are machine-quilted as they are in the other album quilts pictured in this chapter. *Collection of the author*

There are many variety quilts—those made of blocks in multiple patterns or techniques—in the potholder population. The earliest ones generally have either knife-edge finishes (see previous chapters) or narrow bindings around each block, but at the end of the nineteenth century and into the twentieth, a style emerges for bolder colors, chunkier patchwork patterns, and bright bindings that are sometimes wider than those found on the earlier quilts. I documented six quilts either dated or with inferred dates between 1896 and 1920. Three of these are in museum collections, one is in private hands, and two were found on eBay. All are made of many different block patterns, and the colors in the patchwork trend toward Turkey red, indigo blue, and green. Only one is inscribed with enough information to sort the makers, and one of the eBay quilts has place names and initials, but there is not enough information to inform us of their purpose. The blocks are large and, in five examples, bound with Turkey-red binding. The sixth quilt is bound in white; it is from Sanbornville, New Hampshire.

A variety quilt given to me by Judith Ryder has bright-red binding and an intriguing square with three block letters: WRC. After researching the Sunshine Circle quilt for the following story, I now wonder if this is another quilt made for a women's church group. Could WRC stand for Women's Religious Circle? Or, does it represent the Women's Relief Corps, the adjunct organization to the Grand Army of the Republic? If there were inked inscriptions, they have faded completely.

Detail of the Album Quilt, ca. 1920. The Tulip block and several other blocks are machine-appliquéd as well as machine-quilted.

SUNSHINE CIRCLE QUILT, 1928

Sunshine Circle Quilt, 1928. Members of the Sunshine Circle of the Presbyterian Church, Clinton, Indiana. Cotton, 90" by 76". The quilt was made for Mrs. C. H. Vaughn and presented at the group's Christmas party in 1928. *Collection of the author*

Detail of the Sunshine Circle Quilt. Birdella Brown chose an appropriate embroidery pattern for her block.

Detail of the dedicatory block of the Sunshine Circle Quilt

After the publication of Marie Webster's modern quilt designs in 1911, which featured the pastel shades of pink, blue, peach, and green, quilters began to abandon Turkey red and indigo blue. By the 1920s, the softer palate was in vogue, and two such variety quilts were documented in this study.

My eBay purchase of a quilt in this style led to an education in the workings of the Presbyterian Church in Clinton, Indiana. The quilt has an embroidered center square with a dedication to Mrs. C. H. Vaughn from the Sunshine Circle Class, Christmas, 1928. Each of the thirty blocks has a unique signature. Every block is embroidered with the name of the maker, and the peach-colored binding is applied front to back with machine stitching. Twenty-seven of the blocks are machine-quilted, and three are quilted by hand.

There is no good online source for a comprehensive definition of a Sunshine Circle class, because the organization can vary from church to church and region to region. After posting a query on the American Quilt Study Group's Facebook page, I received good information from women who were third-generation members of a Sunshine Circle and women whose mothers or grandmothers were active. Laura Lane, collections manager at the New England Quilt Museum, was involved in her Presbyterian church when she was living in Pennsylvania. A brief interview with her yielded the knowledge that such "circles" are common in churches across the country, and a church may have many women's circles with various names. All are intended to connect women in the church through social and educational programs.[99]

To discover where the quilt was made, I transcribed all the names into an Excel spreadsheet and then started my research with Mrs. C. H. Vaughn. Several towns popped up as possible locations, so I chose two more names and kept searching until all three names appeared in one town, Clinton, Indiana, in the 1940 census.[100]

When I googled "Clinton, Indiana, Sunshine Circle," the *Daily Clintonian* of 1935 yielded monthly activity reports of the Sunshine Circle Class, and several of the quilt signers appeared in these accounts of Bible classes, charitable fundraising, and meetings to organize holiday events. Mrs. H. C. Vaughn was still active, as were several of the other women. Even more informative was the Clinton city directory of 1926. Twenty-seven of the quilt block makers were listed, and I found all but one of the rest of them in the 1932 city directory.[101]

Detail of the Sunshine Circle Quilt. One maker chose to adorn her block with a self-portrait.

Detail of the Dresden Plate Quilt. This quilt is one of only two documented with black binding.

New-Fashioned Quilts

Made in the old-fashioned way

Grandmother used to make quilts so the family could sleep warm. And in spite of today's electric-blanket trend, the enthusiasm for quilted spreads stays just as high. You cherish family quilts because of the nostalgic memories the fabrics bring, or make new ones to preserve memories for the future.

You can design your own quilts around a basic block pattern. By arranging the identical blocks in different positions as you sew them together, you get complete changes in the all-over design. And by changing colors, or using printed cottons, you get still more varied effects.

The two patchwork designs on the opposite page show a few of the many changes you can make with one block design. By experimenting, you can design even more patterns.

If you're short on space for setting up a quilting frame, you'll be interested in the applique block shown below. You can quilt the whole spread, a block at a time. Take it to club meeting, and work on it as you would on your knitting.

You trace the quilting design on a finished block. Pad each block with quilting cotton, then cut a muslin lining the size of your block. Baste the three layers together with long, running stitches. (Put these basting rows four to six inches apart, just close enough so that the cotton batting won't slip around.) Now you're ready to quilt the block by hand.

Bind each block with a strip of bias, either in plain muslin, or a color repeated from the applique. Then sew all the blocks together with a fine whip stitch. Be sure to use strong thread.

Designed by Lucy Pfeiffer

Color Drawings: Kramer-Miller

Tulip Patch applique—You can quilt one block at a time. Bind each block with a bias band, repeating color of tulips. Sew together with a fine whip stitch. Makes an interesting block design on back side, too.

This clipping of the Tulip Patch Quilt designed by Lucy Pfeiffer appeared in the March 1950 *Farm Journal* and *Farmer's Wife Pattern Booklet.* Note the instructions in the last paragraph, to bind each block with a strip of bias, then sew all the blocks together with a fine whipstitch. *Courtesy of Susan Miller*

Most of the women were listed with their husbands or as widows, but several had careers, including retail workers, bookkeepers, accountants, and teachers. The signers' husbands included the minister of the church, superintendents in local businesses, a weigh master, a pasteurizer, and five coal miners.

According to the Clinton, Indiana, city directory published in 1926, it was known as "one of the leading coal producing centers and the liveliest business town in Indiana." At the time it was the largest city in Vermillion County, just north of Terre Haute. It is 160 miles south of Chicago, and in 1920 the population was 10,962.

With the change in palette came different patterns, and again, potholder quilts reflect the use of some of the most popular new ones. I documented two Dresden Plate quilts, as well as two cotton crazy quilts with 1920s and 1930s fabrics. The multipetaled "plates" in both quilts are decorated with black blanket stitch embroidery, part of the popular treatment of appliquéd motifs.

THE LITTLE WOMEN QUILT

Marion Cheever Whiteside Newton was a Boston-born, Paris-trained artist who also loved needlework and designed more than fifty appliqué patterns for quilts, beginning in 1940. She published her patterns in various ladies' magazines as part of her multifaceted business copyrighted as Story Book Quilts. She also produced kits for making quilts of her patterns, managed a large cottage industry of appliqué artists and hand quilters for selling finished quilts, and took commissions from movie stars and American presidents.[102]

Newton developed original patterns based on hundreds of favorite story sources, from Louisa May Alcott to fairy tales and the Bible. The Little Women quilt pattern was one of the most popular, and I have seen many offered for sale by dealers and online auctions, and they all are set with alternating blocks of printed cottons. Two in the New England Quilt Museum collection are set this way. I was surprised to find a Little Women quilt made in potholder fashion, and more surprised to see it without the setting blocks recommended by the designer.

Little Women Quilt, ca. 1960. Unknown maker. Collected in Iowa. Cotton, 85" by 72". Marion Cheever Whiteside Newton's pattern for the Little Women quilt was one of her most popular. *Collection of DeAnn Leiting*

Detail of the Little Women Quilt

PILLOW AND ENVELOPE QUILTS

Envelope quilts became popular in the 1950s after the publication of several versions of a pattern that called for cutting squares of fabric, folding them in half over batting, turning in the edges, and sewing those edges closed. The triangles were then sewn together in patchwork patterns (or not), producing a two-sided quilt. Four of these folded envelope quilts were brought to my attention by members of the Potholder Posse; I was given one and I purchased one. Two had large triangles, measuring 5 inches or more on the sides of the right triangle, and the rest were smaller, measuring just 3 inches. A pair of boxes of an unfinished project also found its way into my collection, complete with the maker's notes on the numbers of blocks she needed to complete the quilt and the amount of wadding, or batting, she needed and a collection of pieces in various stages of completion.

Other pillow quilts were made from small, square pillows. The example in the accompanying image was made in Massachusetts, according to the eBay seller from whom I purchased it. It is made of silk, rayon, and some polyester blends. A source for this pattern or technique has not been found.

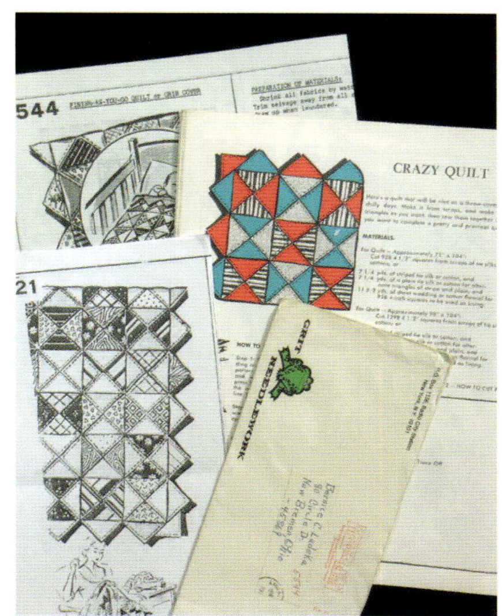

Patterns for envelope quilts were available by mail order and in newspapers and magazines. *Collection of the author*

Not everyone finished their quilts; here is a UFO (unfinished object) in a box. *Collection of the author*

Stack of unfinished envelope blocks. Several sizes were recommended for pillow quilts. *Collection of the author*

Silky Pillows Quilt, ca. 1950. Icle Hankla, Cape Cod, Massachusetts. Silk, blends, 92" by 88". The quilt is constructed of 1,052 3", hand-sewn pillows. *Collection of the author*

Detail of the Silky Pillows Quilt

Two other eBay finds are the 1980s pillow quilts pictured here. In the first edition of the Fannings' book on quilting, they discuss quilt as you go and state that quilts made of pillow blocks date back to the Civil War. I suspect that the *Robbing Peter to Pay Paul* small quilt may have been inspired by this book.[103]

The source of the pattern for the velveteen quilt is not known, but the materials and construction are typical of large quilts of the 1980s, especially those suggested for use on water beds. The pillows are 10 inches square, appliquéd with a chevron motif all in velvet, and embroidered with gold silk. All the pillows are then sewn together to make a huge, heavy bed quilt.

Flat Pillows Quilt, ca. 1970. Unknown maker. Cotton, 44" by 44". *Collection of the author*

Velvet Pillows Quilt, ca. 1980. Unknown maker. Velveteen, 90" by 84". A pattern for this quilt has not yet been found, but its weight would have quelled the waves in any water bed. *Collection of the author*

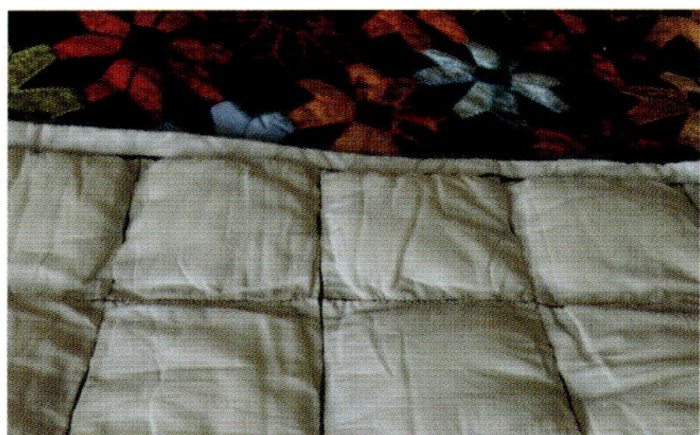

Detail of the *Velvet Pillows* Quilt

Detail of the Velvet Pillows Quilt. The back of the pillows is muslin, and borders are added in the form of long pillows.

Detail of the *F*lat Pillows Quilt

CARL HELLBUSCH POTHOLDER QUILT

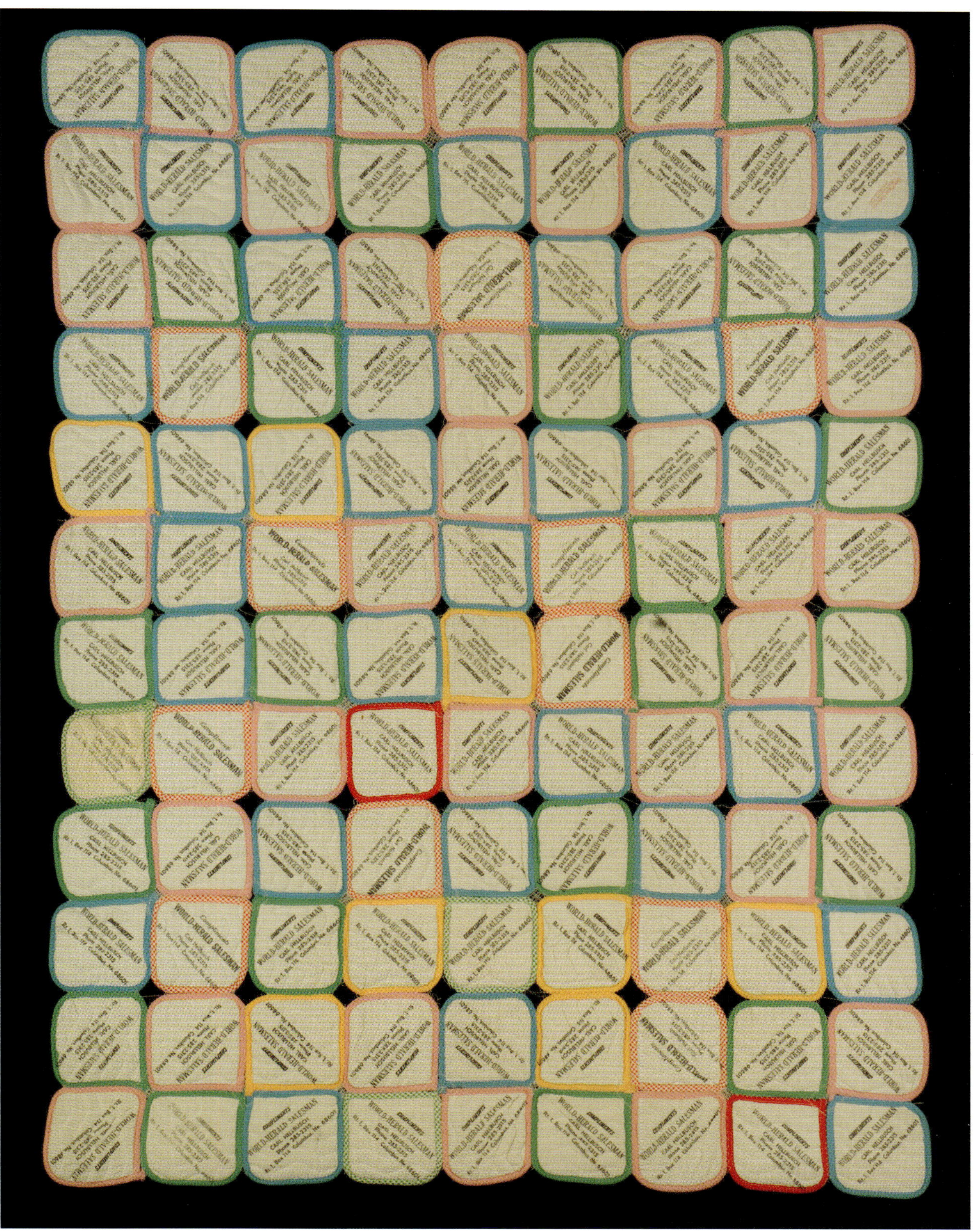

Carl Hellbusch Potholder Quilt. Unknown maker, collected in Texas. Cotton, 66" by 49". Carl Hellbusch was a salesman for the *Omaha World-Herald* and most likely used the potholders as premiums. Look carefully and you will see that one potholder on the left edge was employed for its original purpose in the kitchen, soiled, washed, and used to finish the quilt. *Collection of the author; photo by David Bohl*

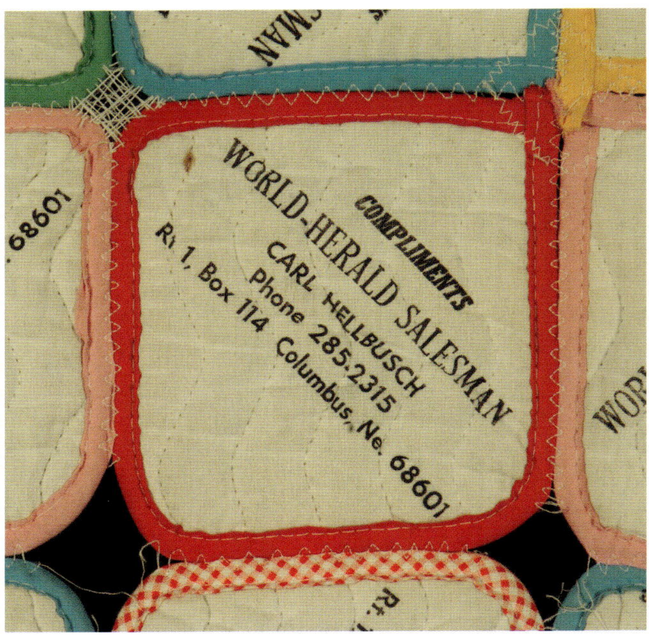

Detail of the Carl Hellbusch Potholder Quilt. The potholders were sewn together rather crudely with a variation on a zigzag stitch, and in some areas, white thread was used in an attempt to cover the large gaps. *Photo by David Bohl*

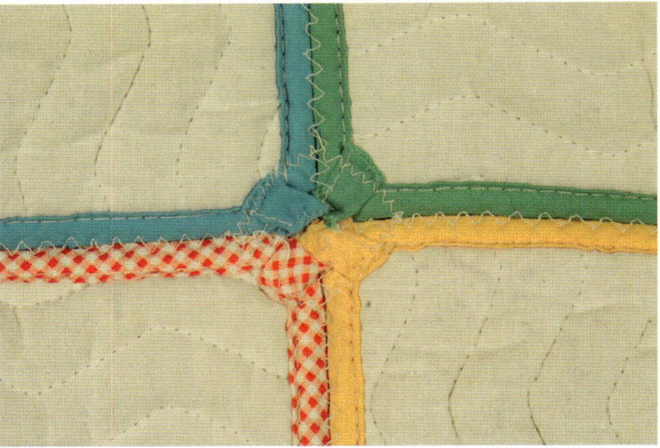

Detail of the Carl Hellbusch Potholder Quilt. Four potholder hanging loops are mashed into submission. *Photo by David Bohl*

A member of the Potholder Posse called from a flea market in Texas to ask if I wanted to buy a potholder quilt constructed of actual potholders. Money was exchanged and a box arrived from a textile dealer with this wonderful example of an overrun of advertising premiums sewn up to make something useful. The quilt can be dated after 1963, the year when zip codes were introduced by the United States Postal Service.

Carl Hellbusch, whose name, address, and phone number are printed on each potholder, was born in eastern Nebraska, living a good part of his life in or near Columbus in Platte County. He was raised in the Lutheran Church, attended Lutheran schools in Nebraska and Missouri, married Dora Hollman in 1938, had three daughters and a son, and was an agent and director of Farmer's Mutual Home Insurance Company. He sold subscriptions for the rural *Omaha World-Herald* newspaper, from which this information is gleaned. It is likely that he sold subscriptions to women who would consider the potholders useful. Did he or his wife have an excess of the promotional potholders and make a quilt? Notice that one potholder on the left edge of the quilt was put to use before it was washed and included in the quilt.

Detail of the Gammy Elder Potholder Quilt. *Photo by David Bohl*

Gammy Elder Potholder Quilt, 1915. Harriet Eva St. Clair Strong Elder, Portland, Rhode Island. Cotton, 104" by 83". According to family legend, the quilt was probably made for a wedding present in the first quarter of the twentieth century. However, the author believes the blocks are earlier and were made into a quilt in the early twentieth century. *Collection of Polly Mello; photo by David Bohl*

CHAPTER 8

QUICK AND EASY QUILTING: 1970 INTO THE TWENTY-FIRST CENTURY

Quilt historians vary in their opinions about the rise and fall of quilting in this country.

A common belief is that the first revival started in 1876, when the United States Centennial Exhibition in Philadelphia featured hundreds of quilts, reviving an interest in colonial crafts. Others recognize only two revivals, one at the beginning of the twentieth century, when designers offered nature-based patterns in a freshened pastel palette, and a second spurred by the US bicentennial in 1976. Another opinion is that the revival has been one long one, ebbing and flowing since the 1870s. Stimulated by the Arts and Crafts movement and the availability of fabrics manufactured in this country, it then stalled during wartimes, while women did other work, and grew in popularity after WWII with increased leisure time.[104]

A back-to-the-land movement in the late 1960s created an interest in the "old" crafts, including quilting. Jean Ray Laury published her first book on quilting in 1966 and as editor at *Better Homes and Gardens* oversaw increasing coverage of quilting and patterns.[105] Other magazines followed suit, but more than one author observed a resistance to the craft due to the time it took to make a bed-sized quilt and the amount of space that a quilting frame took.[106] Perhaps in response, *Quilter's Newsletter Magazine* published a series of articles on quilt as you go, with the first appearing in 1972.

Bonnie Leman was the founder and editor of *Quilter's Newsletter Magazine*, and her 1972 book *Quick and Easy Quilting* was one of the earliest and most comprehensive. She wrote: "They are reluctant to begin because they feel quilting takes too much space, too much time, and too much trouble. I hope this book will show that quilting can be picked up and carried around as easily as knitting, crocheting, or needlepoint."[107]

Publishing companies picked up on the 1970s craft revival, and a review of quilting books from the 1970s to early 1980s suggests that everyone was trying to get a book out on quick-and-easy quilting. Most of the books on machine quilting and quilt as you go from this period provide instructions for the novelty methods explained in chapter 1, including biscuit quilts, cathedral window, and yo-yo quilts. "Stuff and puff" appears in a few, and the technique is also called "pillow quilts."[108] Fabric squares are sewn face together, turned, and then filled with polyester stuffing (not the flat batting produced for making two-dimensional quilts, but the filling used for soft-toy making) and the opening sewn closed (see the quilt on page 142). The squares are then sewn together. Some books suggest embellishing the squares before sewing, turning, and stuffing, while others direct the maker to select a patchwork pattern and work up squares, rectangles, or triangles (or a combination); stuff them; and then sew them together in the chosen pattern.

The 1970s saw a flurry of books published about quilt as you go and "quick-and-easy quilting," and the technique is experiencing a revival. *Collection of the author*

The Ramsey Family Quilt, 1971–73. Made by Bets Ramsey. Cotton, 67" by 47". Bets made this "Add a Block" quilt by binding individually constructed and randomly sized blocks. Each block symbolizes important events or places. *Photo by Richard H. Connors*

The Ramsey Family Quilt

I came to quilt making after ten years in a career as a textile artist when, in 1971, I took a graduate school seminar on the history of crafts in America. My topic was quilt making. During the course I used Florence Ickies's *The Standard Book of Quilt Making* and taught myself to quilt. I studied the few books available at that time on the processes, techniques, and traditions of quilt making and its history.

Among other bits of information, I learned that quilt makers a century earlier had used a method of joining together small, finished blocks to make a whole quilt. This has become known as the potholder technique. Later, Georgia Bonesteel was recognized for this style of quilt as you go through her TV series.

I was eager to try anything, and this seemed like a good way to start putting together a quilt. I was already doing appliqué, so I made an image of my house on a background material, added a piece of outing flannel as batting, and put a backing to it, turning the edges over to the front as birding. Then I quilted it. I soon learned that flannel did not allow the quilting to stand out as bas-relief. I made several other pieces in the same way, using regular quilt batting, and whipped the edges of the adjoining blocks together on the back.

I did not have an overall plan, thinking someday I would have a quilt to cover the bed, but I enjoyed making a block every so often to add to the whole. I incorporated family items: birth states, houses, colleges, sports, travel, hobbies, and pets. The quilt kept growing, and I showed it to some of my friends, including Doris Hoover, a well-known California artist. She said, "Just leave the quilt the way it is, with its irregular sides. It has more interest that way," so leave it I did in 1973, and immediately I had several opportunities to exhibit it in quilt shows in the Southeast, especially at Arrowmont School in Gatlinburg. It has been featured in exhibitions many times since that first outing.

—Bets Ramsey

In a 1977 issue of *Woman's Day Magazine*, Marti Michell's article "The Quickest Quilt in the World" promoted a quilt as you go technique she first called stitch and flip (eventually renamed Quilt-as-You-Piece) that eliminated the need for a quilting frame. The quilt was offered in a kit with five different colorways, and over the next five years hundreds of thousands were sold to people who wanted to make a quilt quickly.[109] Michell developed many techniques for making large quilts in smaller sections and offered several methods for joining them.

Detail of log cabin QAYG, ca. 1980. Unknown maker. Cotton. The author found this lovely little example of quilt as you go on eBay. *Collection of the author*

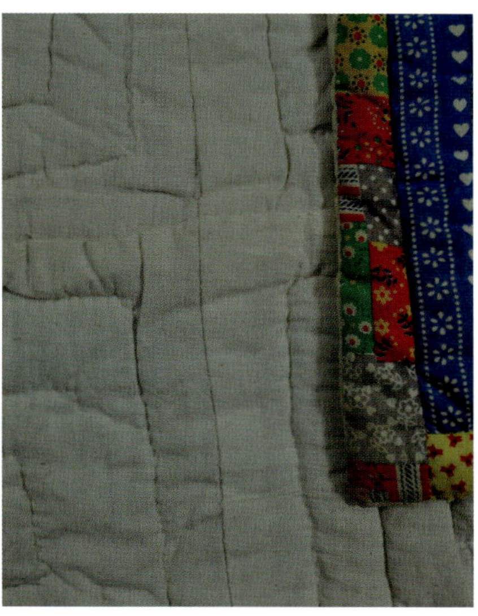

Detail of log cabin QAYG. Note the shadow of the edges of the back of the blocks, where they have been folded over and sewn down by hand.

Georgia Bonesteel published her first book, *Lap Quilting*, in 1982, and whenever I mention quilt as you go, most people ask, "Oh, like Georgia Bonesteel?" I explain that she didn't invent it, but she was very good at promoting the technique through her nationally broadcast television show and her many books. I searched her books to learn how she developed the process, and found that she did not learn "lap quilting" from anyone. While living in New Orleans in the 1960s and 1970s, she made and sold handbags that she embroidered and quilted in 10-by-24-inch squares, holding them in her lap, and then transforming those squares into bags. When she moved to Flat Rock, North Carolina, in 1972, she started teaching quilting. She designed a class in which everyone in the class would piece a quilt and then group-quilt it so that each person would go home with a finished quilt. It did not work out that way, and so she redesigned the class and had folks finish their work by quilting them in sections and then joining them. At first, she had students sew the tops of the sections together, but then changed it so that her students would sew the backs on the machine and do the handwork on the top. She had heard of apartment quilting, perhaps from Ruby McKim, and renamed the technique lap quilting.[110]

Georgia Bonesteel quickly became one of the rock stars of quilt as you go with her television series and many books on lap quilting. *Courtesy of Georgia Bonesteel*

Many of us who took up quilting in the 1970s were enrolled in adult education classes at community colleges. We were taught how to draft patterns and templates, hand- and machine-piece, hand-quilt in sections, and join those sections using quilt as you go techniques. We were not encouraged to machine-quilt; machine quilting was looked down upon and was not considered acceptable until well after 1989, when Caryl Bryer Fallert won a national award for her machine-pieced and machine-quilted masterpiece, *Solar Eclipse*. The slow rise of machine quilting in sections was fueled by the publication of how-to books. The Fannings published a revised edition of *The Complete Book of Machine Quilting* in 1995, which offered nine ways to join machine-quilted sections to make a larger quilt.

A large number of quilts were made in the 1970s and 1980s by using the various quilt as you go techniques, and I documented several, including the two that I made for family members. There is a resurgence of interest in the concept, and a quick search on Amazon.com yielded three titles published in the last three years, including *Quilt as You Go Handbook by* Pauline Rogers and two by Jera Brandvig—*Quilt as-You-Go Made Modern* and *Quilt as-You-Go Made Vintage*. From informal surveys conducted at quilt guilds when I presented on QAYG, I learned that some hobbyists are taking it up in response to the rising cost of professional longarm quilting services. In a quick survey of Facebook groups formed on the topic of Quilt As You Go!, the largest group has 112,000 members as of February 2021, and the other two have a combined 52,000 members. On YouTube, there are hundreds of tutorials on many methods for QAYG.

Wendy Reed, a prolific maker of marvelous potholder quilts, is a pioneer in getting major quilt shows to accept this technique. She entered the American Quilter's Society competition as early as 2010 and won a second-place ribbon for appliqué at the Road to California show in 2012. She has also won multiple first-place ribbons at the Vermont Quilt Festival. When asked if she received judges' comments on the binding style, she laughed and said, "Yes, I always get full points for my bindings—all of them."[111] Wendy went on to say this:

> My quilt-making journey began more than fifty years ago, but I did not discover the potholder method until the early 1980s. After my first attempt at this form of construction, I was hooked. I quilt every day, and the portability of this method allows me more quilting time because I can take my projects anywhere. I believe my fascination with the potholder method stems from the fact that I love small things in tidy little packages. My favorite step in the process is when I have all my individual "quiltlets" neatly piled up waiting to be stitched together. By sharing the tricks and tips I have learned with other quilters, I feel that I am helping to keep this historic method alive.[112]

Pan Blackened Appliqué, 2019. Wendy Reed, Bath, Maine. Cotton, 47" by 36". Wendy Reed is a potholder quilt master maker, winning awards at large regional quilt shows. *Collection of the artist*

Detail of the Pan Blackened Appliqué

Cynthia Black made a scaled-down version of the Martha Fuller, Bristol, Maine, quilt in the collection of the Maine State Museum. She drafted the patterns and finished each block individually. She explained:

> I had looked for a while for a quilt to replicate in miniature for the challenge at Maine Quilts, and nothing "spoke" to me until I saw the 1840s Bristol quilt. Since I had not yet made a potholder quilt, this was the perfect opportunity to do so! Enjoyed drafting the patterns and searching for appropriate fabrics for each block! Am amazed at the complex designs the ladies made![113]

No Bake Appliqué, 2014. Wendy Reed, Bath, Maine. Cotton, 78" by 60". *Collection of the artist*

Detail of the No Bake Appliqué

Martha Fuller Reproduction Quilt, 2018. Cynthia Black, Litchfield, Maine. Cotton, 45.5" by 39.5". For a challenge, Cynthia Black chose to reproduce the Martha Jane Fuller quilt in the collection of the Maine State Museum. Both were exhibited in 2018 at the Pine Tree Quilt Show in Augusta, Maine. *Collection of the artist*

Donald Beld, my coauthor of *Civil War Quilts*, was a lover of all things Civil War and an avid maker of potholder quilts. He founded the Home of the Brave Project, in which volunteers from all over the country made quilts to present to the family members of soldiers who died in the Iraq or Afghanistan conflicts. Thousands of quilts were made during the life of the project, which is now officially discontinued. An offshoot of this was his Fallen Heroes project. Again, state by state Don enlisted volunteers to help make 8-inch blocks to memorialize service people who died in these conflicts. Each block was made with Civil War reproduction fabrics, and most were nine-patch blocks. The face of the block contained the patchwork and the name and service branch of the deceased soldier. The reverse contained information or stories about the soldier. There are eleven Fallen Heroes quilts now in the New England Quilt Museum collection, and some are put on display for Memorial Day and Veteran's Day each year.

Detail of the Martha Fuller Reproduction Quilt

Martha Jane Fuller Quilt, ca. 1840. Various makers, South Bristol, Maine. Cotton, 78" by 67". *Courtesy of the Maine State Museum, 70.109.1*

Don Beld's Gift, 2012. Donald Beld, Riverside, California. Cotton. The Civil War reproduction quilt comprises many of the blocks given as patterns in the book *Civil War Quilts* by Pamela Weeks and Don Beld. This was a gift to Pam from Don and was so typical of his generous spirit. *Collection of the author*

Donald Beld founded the Fallen Heroes project to make a block honoring each service person who died in the conflicts in Iraq or Afghanistan. Don speaks to the author about the project as he presents the Fallen Heroes Quilt Number 4, Nebraska, to the New England Quilt Museum.

Detail of Alphabetically Speaking, 2005. Pat LaPierre, Naples, Florida. Cotton, 23" by 18". This is one of the early quilts made block by block in which Pat perfected her machine quilting. *Collection of the artist*

Several art quilters are making potholder quilts, both two-dimensional and three-dimensional. Pat LaPierre's machine quilting has won her awards at large regional quilt shows, and she often works block by block to achieve her intricate designs. Her 2002, two-sided quilt *Elusive Castle* won a third-place ribbon at the American Quilter's Society competition in Paducah, Kentucky. *Elusive Castle* is pieced from fabrics Pat collected as part of a Y2K internet fabric exchange. She pieced four-patch blocks; created square, flat pillows; and set them on point at the corners. The opposing side is created in the same way, and each unit is a small button-covered quilt.

Civil War Quilts featured a large how-to section on potholder quilts. Because it was published in time for the 150th anniversary of the start of the American Civil War and enjoyed wide sales, interest in making quilts block by block increased. In 2011, I was guest curator

Detail of the Elusive Castle, 2002. Pat LaPierre, Naples, Florida. Cotton, 58" by 86". A Y2K internet exchange yielded 2,000 different fabrics for this quilt. *Collection of the artist*

Rising Water, 2006. Mary Beth Bellah, Charlottesville, Virginia. Cotton, plastic, 28" by 48" by 38". Mary Beth works with rectangles reinforced with plastic armatures to create three-dimensional installations. *Collection of the artist*

at the New England Quilt Museum of an exhibit of quilts made potholder style. Don and I presented at quilt guilds and historical associations, and within a short time after the publication of *Civil War Quilts*, at least two or three people at my lectures had heard of them. People began bringing their potholder quilts to show me, and several guilds in New England and New York have made them for presentation or raffle quilts.

I hope you will keep your eyes out for antique and vintage examples as you visit museums and antique shops and let me know when you find one. When you have a minute, try making a small one. Whip up a few blocks or take out your orphan blocks, bind them, and spend an evening sewing them together. Like Wendy Reed and many of us, you might get hooked!

The director of the New England Quilt Museum in Lowell, Massachusetts, invited the author to curate an exhibit of potholder quilts in 2011. The exhibit included quilts from 1838 to 2010.

Genesee Valley Friendship Quilt, 2019. Made by members of the Genesee Valley Quilt Club, Rochester, New York. Cotton, silk, 91" by 91". Christine Wickert organized this gorgeous quilt for the group's annual raffle. *Private collection; photo by David Braitsch*

It Takes a Village, 2013. Kathy Mulberger, Bethlehem, Pennsylvania. Cotton, 48" by 48". Kathy had a stack of blocks from a family block exchange. After she read the author's 2012 article on potholder quilts, she started by binding each block, joined them, and then chose to add borders. *Collection of the artist; photo by Kelsi Krebs*

Hexagon Quilt, 2016. Rhonda Dort, Houston, Texas. Cotton, silk, embellishments, 36" by 36". Rhonda's hexagon work is centered on recycling vintage textiles that might otherwise be discarded because of damage or staining. *Collection of the artist*

Detail of Rhonda's Hexagon Quilt. Cotton, silk, embellishments. *Collection of the artist*

Kevin's Wool Potholder Quilt, 2011. Cindy Thury Smith, Hastings, Minnesota. Cotton, flannel, wool, 80" by 48". Cindy developed the concept of using the printed part of a T-shirt for the center of each block, adding strips of flannel or wool, and binding each block. *Collection of the artist*

Hanging by a Thread

Challenge a group of quilters to try self-portraiture and what do you get? Here's an award-winning example from the Washington State group Hanging by a Thread. The quilt took nearly two years to complete, and one portrait even survived a flood. Each quiltmaker chose a focus color and used the techniques in Marilyn Belford's 2006 self-published book, *Portraits for Fabric Lovers*.

90 QUILTERS NEWSLETTER • AUGUST/SEPTEMBER 2009

Hanging by a Thread, 2009. Made by members of the group Hanging by a Thread, Washington State. Cotton. The group was challenged to make a portrait quilt, and each produced a finished block. The black mounting sections have finished edges, and self-portraits are stitched to these. The quilt won first place in the group category at the International Quilt Festival in Houston, Texas, in 2009. *Collection of the group of artists*

Butterfly Add-a-Block, 2018. Pamela Weeks, Auburn, New Hampshire. Cotton, 51" by 45". When confronted with a pile of blocks from vintage quilts, the author chose to make a potholder quilt. *Collection of the artist*

LeDuc Civil War Potholder Quilt, 2011. Evening Star Quilters of Red Wing and the Spiral Piecemakers of Hastings, Minnesota. Cotton, 85" by 49". Cindy Thury Smith organized the making of the quilt and is the curator of the Hastings Pioneer Room, where the quilt is displayed. *Courtesy of the Hastings Pioneer Room, Hastings, Minnesota*

English Exotic Hexagon Quilt, ca. 1980. This quilt is another eBay find and a wonderfully weird piece that the seller stated was English. The hexagon blocks are pieced of silks or home decoration fabrics. Each hexagon is then edged with a form of blanket stitch, and needle weaving is used to join them. The borders are joined to the main body of the quilt with crochet. *Collection of the author*

Detail of the English Exotic Hexagon Quilt. *Collection of the author*

CHAPTER 9

QUILT AS YOU GO PROJECTS

GENERAL INSTRUCTIONS

The small projects presented here are examples of four of the many ways to make quilts in sections before joining them to make larger quilts. The shortcut techniques used to piece these units are not discussed here. I encourage you to use these as jumping-off places and design your own quilts, adapting them as your creativity directs.

Fabric amounts are given assuming you are purchasing new cotton fabrics (or dipping into your stash) and that they are 40" wide. The amounts are generous, which allows for a few mistakes in cutting and leaves you with more scraps for the next project. All the projects are flexible in fabric use, and the smaller pieces can be cut from larger scraps. It is all up to you.

NOTE: These projects are great for using scraps or dipping into your fat-quarter stash; fat quarters are generally cut 18 by 22 inches and sold that way in quilt shops.

Instructions are for rotary cutting, and the dimensions of each piece include a ¼" seam allowance. Generally, cut strips of fabric the desired size and then cut these into the pattern pieces needed. For example, if you need thirty-six 2" squares, cut 2" strips across the length of the fabric and then cut the strips into squares.

There are several blocks with square units made of triangles. The shortcut techniques used to piece these units are not discussed here. It may be worth your time to investigate speedy ways to piece half-square triangles if you are inclined.

Set up your sewing machine for accurate piecing by placing a ruler on your machine so that the needle hits a ¼" marking with the edge of the ruler to the right of the needle, then place a piece of tape at that edge to mark your seam allowance. Or, use a ¼" presser foot. Practice with scraps of fabric until you can stitch an accurate ¼" seam.

If you choose to hand-piece Briar's Baby Quilt or Aunt Jo's Gift, you can still rotary-cut, remembering to sew ¼" inside the cut line, or make templates based on the measurements given for each piece.

FINISHING POTHOLDER QUILT BLOCKS

BINDING

Many nineteenth-century quilts were finished with bindings that started on one corner of the quilt, wound all the way around it, and finished back at the start. Today, we are generally careful to start on a side of the quilt, make perfectly mitered corners, and hide the binding join, using a method beautifully illustrated in Harriet Hargrave's *The Art of Classic Quiltmaking*. I like to use a combination of the two methods by starting at one corner of a block, mitering each corner, and ending at the beginning corner by turning under the edge of the binding. It saves time, and because the blocks are sewn together, it is barely noticeable.

Potholder quilt blocks are individually bound with single-thickness binding strips. Cut the binding strip for each block 1¼" wide. To calculate the length needed, take four times the measurement of the side of the finished block plus 4". (If your block finishes at 8½", multiply by four. That equals 34", plus 4" totals 38".)

Hint: It is easier to attach binding when using the walking foot on your sewing machine.

Here is a method that creates three perfectly mitered corners but begins and ends the binding on the first corner as seen in many nineteenth-century potholder blocks. Place the finished and trimmed block faceup on your sewing machine table and lay one end of the single-layer binding facedown on one edge at the upper corner. Pin in place. Put one pin at the end of the first edge, ¼" from the edge. You will stop stitching at the pin placement and take three to four backstitches.

Take the block out of the machine and snip the threads.

Give the block a quarter turn to the left, so that the strip you just sewed is on the "top" of the block away from you. Take the unsewn binding strip in your right hand and fold it up and away from the block, creating a fold at 45 degrees, then fold the strip back down to cover the next side of the block, being careful to maintain the fold you just created by pinning it in place. This new fold will be parallel to the upper edge of the block.

Start sewing at the edge of the block and remember

1. Lay a binding strip on one side of the block and pin. Set a stopping pin ¼" from the end and sew to that pin. Stop, backstitch, and remove the block from the sewing machine.

2. Fold the binding strip up to make a 45-degree angle.

4. Before sewing the final side, stop to finger-press the strip at the starting point over to the back, turning under the raw edge, and pin in place.

3. Keeping the angle, fold the strip down, pin, and sew to the next stopping pin.

to place your next "stopping pin" ¼" from the bottom edge. Repeat the procedure on two more corners of the block, for a total of three mitered corners. Before you place the block under the needle on the third corner, while the piece is still out of the machine, go to the starting point and finger-press the binding up and over the edge of the block.

On the back, turn under the edge. Pin it in place from the top so that you can easily pull the pin and not stitch over it.

With the block still out of the machine, lay the remainder of the binding strip along that last edge of the block, and cut it ¼" longer than you need to finish the block. Turn under the end so that the strip is the same length as the edge of the block, and pin in place.

Finish stitching the last edge, turn the binding over, turn under the edges, and sew down by hand, using a blind stitch. You may sew it by machine, but the quilt will be a bit stiffer.

FOLDED-UP BACKING FINISH (BACKING BROUGHT TO FRONT)

While working on the Add a Block project, I found this quick and easy way to finish the edges of the blocks. The provided measurements result in an edge finish of ¼", so if you prefer a wider finish, adjust accordingly.

Prepare the finished block by pressing, layering it with batting, and cutting the backing at least 1½" larger all around than the block. Quilt the block. Trim the backing to a generous ¾". Using a ruler with a 45-degree angle, trim the backing at each corner, leaving ¼" (see illustration). Press all of the backing under ¼". Fold the sides over the edges of the block and pin in place, being careful to make a neat join at each corner. Stitch in place by hand or machine.

Block finished by turning backing brought to front

Pillow layers prepared for sewing

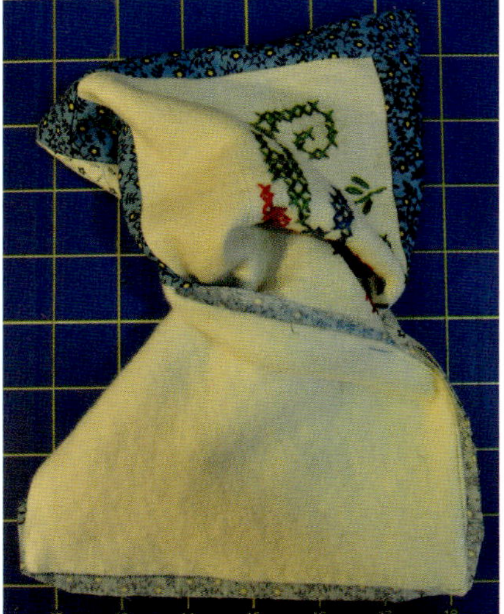

Pillow block after trimming, beginning turning right side out

PILLOW OR PILLOWCASE FINISH

Blocks finished with this method must either be quilted after the finishing technique or quilted to the batting with no backing. Place the backing right side up and layer the top right side down on the backing, with the batting making the last layer. Pin in place and machine-sew around the assemblage, leaving a 4" opening on one edge. *Note*: For sharp corners, stop the machine, needle down, just before the corner, and take two to three stitches on the diagonal, then continue on the next side.

Once all sides are sewn, trim the seam allowance and cut across the corners close to the diagonal stitching, reducing the bulk as much as possible, especially at the corners. Draw the layers through the opening and use a knitting needle, skewer, or point turner to poke the corners from the inside, making them as sharp as possible. Turn in the seam allowance at the opening and sew closed by hand. You may choose to topstitch the block ¼" from the edges to prevent the backing from rolling to the front.

KNIFE-EDGE FINISH

This is the fiddliest of the finishes, and one that I use the least, but here's the easiest way I can figure out how to manage it. The majority of the quilts with blocks that are finished knife edge have the thinnest batting possible, and if you can possibly split the batting, or be happy using a prewashed cotton flannel for filling, do so. Be sure to leave an inch or two unquilted near the edges of the block—the more room you leave for turning under the edges, the easier it is. You can always go back and add quilting once the edges are finished.

Trim the block—top and backing—¼" larger than the desired finished size all around. Trim the batting back by ½". With the right side of the block facing up on an ironing surface, fold back the top of the block and the batting, pinning if necessary to hold them in place. Fold, then press the backing up ¼". Repeat on all sides. Turn the block over and repeat with the fabric of the top, making sure the folded edges meet. Baste the edges closed, then use the ladder stitch to securely close the edges of the block.

Block finished knife edge, pressed, pinned, and stitching begun

Block finished by turning up backing and placing top layer on it, with edges turned under

The back of the Add a Block Quilt, showing machine zigzag joining

TOP APPLIED TO TURNED-UP BACKING

The two English quilts (page 115) in this book are composed of multiple-sized blocks made by this method, and they do not contain batting. I used this method for one piece in the Add a Block project, since the embroidered piece was already hemmed, and that hem was too small to undo and finish in any other way.

Cut the backing 1" larger than the finished size all around. Place the backing right side down, and if you are using it, place the batting cut to the finished size onto the wrong side of the backing. Then fold up each edge of the backing over the batting, mitering the corners. Baste or pin in place. Turn under the edges of the block top and place it over the backing and sew it in place by machine or hand. See the bottom left image on page 115.

JOINING POTHOLDER BLOCKS

Potholder blocks are most often sewn together from the back with a whipstitch or overcast stitch, with small stitches placed close together in a neutral thread color or one that matches the binding color. The stitching must be dense, or the blocks will sag or separate. Wendy Reed, in finishing her contemporary quilts, uses a ladder stitch, which is completely hidden in the binding fabric.

I've worked out a way to sew the blocks together by using a very narrow zigzag stitch on my sewing machine. It works only with applied binding, or one of the back-turned-to-the-front methods, and one must be careful not to stretch the binding too tightly over the edges of the block when applying it.

When enough blocks are finished to begin sewing them together, finger-press the edges of each block to create a crease at the fold. With two blocks face to face, and the sewing machine set up with thread matching the binding, and a narrow, short zigzag stitch, carefully stitch the blocks together. This leaves a slightly deeper "trench" between the blocks on the front of the quilt, but it is so much quicker than hand sewing.

The back of the Add a Block Quilt, showing hand overcast or whipstitch joining

BRIAR'S BABY QUILT

Briar's Baby Quilt, made by Pamela Weeks, Auburn, New Hampshire, 2019. Cotton, 44" by 44".
Collection of the maker's granddaughter

This is a small project for quilt as you go. Yes, you could probably piece the top, layer it with batting and backing, and easily get the whole thing through your home sewing machine, but this is a perfect way to try this technique. I made the blocks small, used a large-scale novelty print for the center, and placed two strips of sashing around each block (the borders around a block are called *sashing*). Blocks surrounded by sashing are best suited to this method for quilt as you go.

The project is easy to adapt to any size once you get the technique of quilting each block, leaving unquilted areas large enough to join the blocks easily, and practice lining up the seams. Simply make yourself a chart, sort the piecing, and off you go!

I have given the fabric amounts for using four fabrics but made mine very scrappy, using three different pinks and four different yellows. I do advise you to use the same fabric for piece B, the outer block sashing, because when you join the blocks, it will appear to be one larger piece, especially if you use a small-scale print for this piece.

MATERIALS

- 100% cotton fabrics are best for baby quilts.
- The main, or focus, fabric and the quilt's outside border is a large-scale print: 1 yard.
- The inner sashing fabrics are scrappy. I used four different yellow prints. Total needed: ½ yard.
- The keystones are four different pink fabrics. Total: ¼ yard.
- The outer sashing of each block is a small-scale green print: ½ yard.
- The final border of the quilt is more of the large-scale print; the quantity needed is included above.
- The backing is the green print and a similar yellow one, and I chose to arrange the blocks to form a nine-patch on the back of the little quilt. Needed are nine 14" squares. If your fabric is 42" wide, you need 1¼ yards. If only 40" wide, you can either piece fabric from the 1¼ yards to make 14" squares, or purchase 2 yards total. Another option is to dig into your stash and make a very scrappy back, using nine different prints, or work out something that makes you happy.
- The binding (around the outer edge of the quilt) is the same large-scale novelty print as the outer border, or you may choose a different fabric: ½ yard.
- Cardboard or plastic template material for making a frame for fussy cutting the center of each block, if desired.
- Thread for hand and machine quilting.
- Batting: Purchase a crib-sized batting that is 45" by 60", or use 14' square scraps from your stash; you will need nine of these.
- Fusible web for joining the batting when joining the blocks.

EQUIPMENT

- Rotary cutter, mat, and ruler
- Standard iron and (optional) small iron
- Straight pins
- Safety pins for basting
- Hand-quilting needles (if you choose to hand-quilt the center of the block)
- Sewing machine with piecing foot and walking foot for quilting
- Scissors

PREPARING THE FABRIC AND BATTING

Prepare your fabrics for rotary cutting by pressing and layering them. I cut as many as six layers at a time.

Batting: Cut two strips 4" by 36½", and two strips 4" by 44½". Cut nine 14" squares.

Fabric: The amounts for each pattern piece are given for the entire quilt.

1. From the novelty print used for the outer border top, cut two strips 4" by 36½" and two strips 4" by 44½".

2. From the novelty print, for the block centers (E), cut nine squares 7½" by 7½". If you want to feature motifs of the novelty print in the center of the blocks as shown, it's easiest to make a fussy-cutting template. Cut a 7½" square of cardboard or template plastic, then cut a 7" square from its center. It will be a fragile, but usable, ¼" wide frame. Position this template on your fabric with the motif positioned as desired and trace around the outside of the template, which is your cutting line (the inner edge of the frame is where your seam will be).

3. From a fabric of your choice for the back of the outer border, cut two strips 4" by 36½" and two strips 4" by 44½".

4. For the pink corners (A) of the outer block sashing, cut thirty-six 1½" squares.

5. For the pink corners (C) of the inner block sashing, cut thirty-six 2" squares.

6. For the green outer sashing strips (B), cut thirty-six rectangles 1½" by 10½" .

7. For the yellow inner sashing strips (D) cut thirty-six rectangles 2" by 7½" .

8. For the back of the blocks, cut nine 14" squares.

9. For the binding, cut five 2½" strips across the width (about 44") of the green fabric.

PIECING

Chain piecing makes quilt blocks go together quickly because you assemble all the components at once, press as directed, and then add them in sequence to finish the blocks.

1. For each of the nine E pieces, sew piece D to one side of piece E and then another D on the opposite side of each piece E. Press seams inward.

2. Sew piece C to each end of the remaining eighteen D pieces. Press seams outward.

3. Sew an assembled pieced C/D/C to opposite sides of each of the E pieces, pinning carefully where the seams cross.

4. In the same manner, for each assembled unit, sew piece B to one side and then another piece B to the opposite side. Press seams inward.

5. Sew piece A to each end of the remaining eighteen B pieces.

6. Sew assembled piece A/B/A units to the remaining sides of the block and press outward.

Layer the finished blocks with a 14" square backing and batting and baste the layers, using safety pins or needle and thread.

QUILTING THE BLOCKS

I chose to hand-quilt around the major motif in each block center and then machine-quilt in the ditch on both sides of the inner sashing. You may decide to do the same or hand- or machine-quilt each block as desired. Do not quilt any part of the block beyond the outer edge of the inner sashing! (D)

Make a frame and use it to select a motif for the center block.

Briar's Baby Quilt, block-piecing diagram

ASSEMBLING THE QUILT

Arrange the quilted blocks as you would like them in the quilt. If needed, make yourself a chart with numbers or letters (or both) and label each block in the order it will be added to the quilt.

First, assemble the blocks into rows.

1. Trim the batting and backing to within ½" of the edges of the blocks.

2. Fold back the batting and backing of two block sandwiches, away from the pieced top on the sides where they will be sewn together. The quilting may have distorted the block, so trim the edges straight if needed. Place the two blocks with the right sides together, pin, and sew just the tops together with a ¼" seam.

3. Turn this unit facedown on your ironing surface and press open the seam, being careful not to also press the folded batting and backing. A small travel or craft iron is helpful here.

4. Unpin the batting, leaving the backing folded back, and smooth one layer of batting over the other. Using scissors, carefully cut through both layers of the batting and remove the trimmings. Your cut should result in the batting edges butting up to each other. Cut a piece of the fusible webbing tape to the length needed, lay it over the butted edges of the batting, and carefully bond the batting with the dry iron. (Alternatively, the butted edges of the batting can be thread-basted by hand.)

5. Unfold the backings, first smoothing one side down over the batting and then the other, layering it over the first backing. Fold this top backing under itself, lining up the fold with the seam of the two blocks, which you should be able to feel beneath the batting. Pin, and sew in place by hand, being careful NOT to catch the batting at least 1" from each end of the seam, or you will not be able to sew the rows together. NOTE: Some authors suggest sewing this seam by machine, but I find it makes for a stiffer, less pliable quilt. Your choice.

6. Continue sewing blocks together into three rows.

7. Join the rows as you joined the blocks, carefully pinning back the batting and backing, sewing the tops together, trimming the batting to butt the edges, fusing the batting, and layering the backing over itself, and hand-sewing it in place.

The blocks are quilted, then the top layers are sewn together, the batting is fused, and the backings are sewn over the seams.

The first border is added.

ADDING THE BORDER

The quilt may have changed dimensions during quilting, so measure the center of the quilt and adjust the side border strips to this measurement.

1. Trim the edges of the quilt to within ½" of the edge of the blocks.

2. Lay a short strip of the border top along one side of the row of blocks, right sides together, and on the back of the quilt do the same with the shortest piece of the border-backing fabric, placing it on the back of the quilt, right sides together. Pin carefully, making sure that the edges align with the top of the quilt.

3. Sew through all layers with a ¼" seam.

4. Leaving the top strip in place, open the border-backing fabric and press it away from the body of the quilt. The right side of the quilt and wrong side of this strip should be facing you.

5. Place a short strip of the batting on the wrong side of the border-backing fabric and, using the fusible web, bond it to the batting at the edge of the quilt.

6. Now, smooth the top border fabric over the fused batting and baste in place, using safety pins or needle and thread. All the borders will be added before they are machine-quilted.

7. Repeat steps 2 through 6 on the other side of the quilt.

8. Adjust the measurements for the remaining top border strips on the basis of the quilt as it now is, being careful to add ½" for seam allowance. Repeat the directions above for adding the border strips to the top and bottom sides of the quilt.

FINISHING THE QUILT

1. I chose to use two rows of simple straight stitching to quilt the borders. You may choose something fancier.

2. After quilting the borders, bind the outer edge of the quilt.

3. Add a label, and you are done!

AUNT JO'S GIFT

Aunt Jo's Gift, Joann Weeks Bailey, 2011. Northwood, New Hampshire. Cotton, 34" by 25". *Collection of the author*

My aunt Joann Weeks Bailey has long been my mentor in all things quilting, and she helped me along the potholder quilt journey. In 2009, she made this small wall hanging, block by block, and it periodically hung in her kitchen, rotated in and out with others designed for that space. She gave it to me as this book neared completion, so I would like to share it with you.

Note: This project is great for using up scraps or dipping into your fat-quarter stash. Aunt Jo chose a color scheme based on her binding fabric, which is a small brown print with rust, blue, and beige highlights. Her blocks are pieced with rust, off-white muslin, beiges, golds, greens, and a bit of blue.

To finish Aunt Jo's Gift as a potholder quilt, finish each block, layer with batting, quilt, and bind it. When all of the blocks are quilted and bound, stitch them together to form the quilt.

MATERIALS

High-quality, 100% cotton fabrics are best for quilts.

- The binding fabric is the same for all of the blocks, and
  the other fabrics are chosen from the colors in this fabric. It is an easy way to choose your palette.
- Binding fabric: ½ yard, and more if you use it for some of the pattern pieces
- Rust print fabric(s): ½ yard, 2 fat quarters, or the equivalent in scraps
- Beige/light-print fabric(s): ¾ yard, 3 fat quarters, or the equivalent in scraps
- Green print fabric(s): one fat quarter, or the equivalent in scraps
- Blue print fabric(s): one fat quarter, or the equivalent in scraps
- Solid off-white fabric: 1 yard if using for backings on all the blocks, and this amount provides leftovers for piecing some of the blocks.

(You may make the same choices as listed above or go with all scraps.)

- Cardboard or plastic template material for the appliqué patterns
- Thread for hand or machine quilting
- Batting: Purchase a crib-sized batting that is 45" by 60", or use 9" square scraps from your stash. You'll need twelve 9" squares of batting.

EQUIPMENT

- Rotary cutter, mat, and ruler
- Scissors
- Iron (press fabrics before cutting them)
- Straight pins
- Safety pins for basting before quilting
- Hand-quilting needles (if you choose to hand-quilt the blocks)
- Sewing machine with piecing foot (and free-motion or walking foot for machine quilting if you choose)
- Permanent fabric pen for inscribing the quilt, if desired
- Embroidery floss

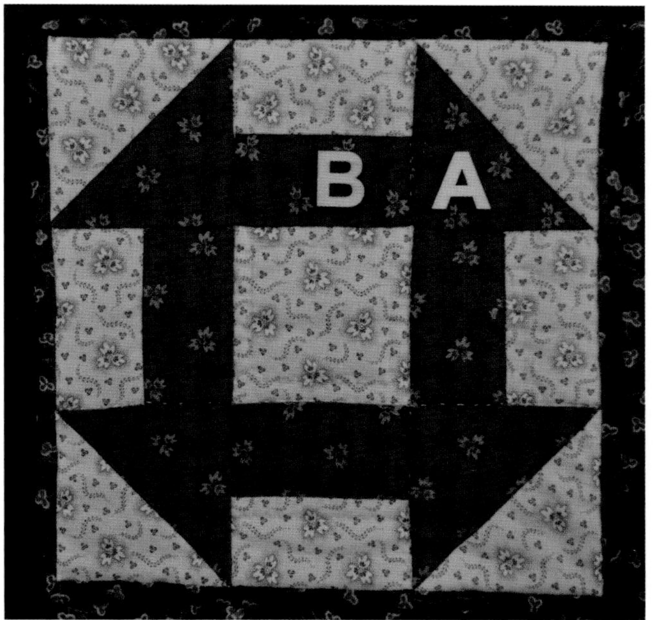

Churn dash

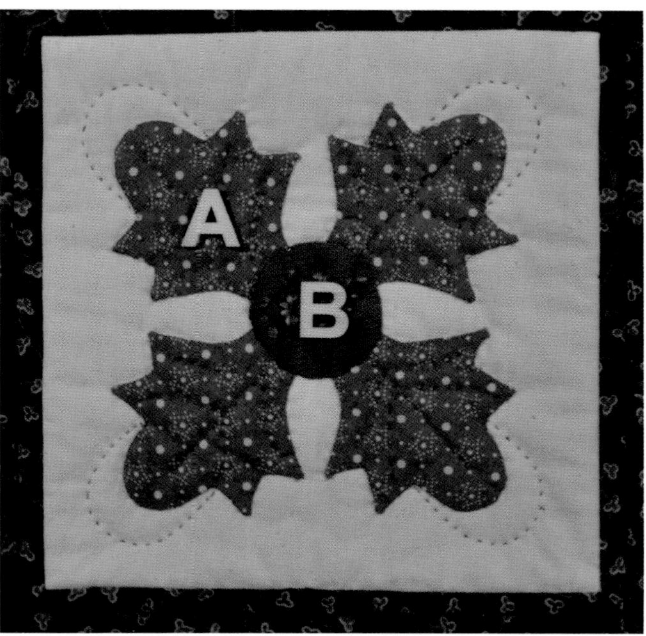

Oak leaf

DIRECTIONS

The patterns were altered so that all the blocks finish 8½" square, with no points being lost to the binding of each block, as seen in Aunt Jo's quilt.

Prepare cardboard or plastic templates for the appliqué shapes you plan to use.

First cut the binding fabric and then cut the fabrics for each block; piece or appliqué as needed.

Aunt Jo inscribed many of the blocks, which you can do using archival permanent pens. To make it easier to write on the fabric, fuse freezer paper to the back of the block to be inscribed. Remove the paper before layering and quilting the block.

After completing the piecing, appliqué, or embroidery in each block, press it well. (Press appliqué from the back, using a towel to cushion the work.)

Layer with batting and backing, baste with safety pins or stitching, and quilt as desired.

Trim the blocks to a common size *after* quilting; the patterns provided here should result in blocks 8½" square, but the quilting may alter that somewhat.

Bind each of the blocks.

Arrange the bound blocks as you wish. Sew them together from the back, place them face to face, and, using a whipstitch, sew them together. First create rows of blocks and then join the rows.

CUTTING AND CONSTRUCTION

From the binding fabric, cut twelve strips 1¼" by 34" across the width of the fabric.

For the backing, you will need to cut twelve 9" squares.

CHURN DASH

For piece A, cut two 3½" squares of dark fabric and two 3½" squares of beige/light fabric. Cut each square in half, diagonally, to yield four triangles of each color.

For piece B, cut four rectangles of each color 1 13/16" by 3 13/16".

For piece C, cut one 3/16" square of the beige/light color.

Sew the beige/light and dark triangles together to form four squares. Then sew the beige/light and dark rectangles together to form four squares. You now have the nine units that make up the block; sew them together as seen in the block.

OAK LEAF APPLIQUÉ

Prepare oak leaf and circle templates for tracing on your fabric (see pattern on page 180).

Cut a 9" square of printed or solid off-white fabric for the background of the block. Fold it in half corner to corner twice and finger-press to make guidelines for the appliqué.

Make templates for the oak leaves and the large circle as seen on the pattern page that follows.

Cut four oak leaves from green fabric and a circle for the center of the rust or dark fabric, remembering to leave at least 1/8" around the traced lines for turning under. Position the leaves evenly on the square and appliqué in place. Appliqué the circle in the center of the block, placing it to cover the bottom edges of the leaves.

Album

Economy patch

ALBUM

For the "arms" (A), cut four rectangles $3\frac{5}{16}$" by 5". Once the block is pieced, you will trim them to make the block square.

For the triangles (B), cut one $5\frac{3}{16}$" square of the beige/light print and then cut this diagonally (corner to corner) twice, resulting in four triangles.

For the center square (C), cut a $3\frac{5}{16}$" square.

Sew A pieces to two opposite sides of the C center square. Sew two B triangles to each side of the two remaining A pieces, being careful to line the pieces up as seen in the block diagram below. Press all seams toward the A pieces. Join the three units, then trim the "arms" so that the block is 9" square.

To construct this block, first sew the B triangles to two of the A pieces, and two A pieces to the center block C. Then sew the three components together, press, and trim as shown.

ECONOMY PATCH

For A, cut two $4\frac{7}{8}$" squares of the beige/light print and cut each square once on the diagonal to yield four triangles. Cut one $4\frac{7}{8}$" square of the solid off-white fabric and cut it once on the diagonal to yield two triangles. You need only one triangle for the center of the block, so discard the other light triangle.

For piece B, cut one $5\frac{3}{16}$" square each of medium-brown, blue, and rust and cut each square on the diagonal twice, yielding four triangles of each color. You need four triangles of the medium brown but only one each of the blue and rust; discard the three extra blue and rust triangles.

Sew the blue and rust triangles together on the short side, press the seam open, then sew this unit to the light-colored A triangle.

Now sew the four B triangles to this center unit, press the seams open, and sew the four A triangles to this larger unit. Inscribe the center triangle as desired.

Ohio star

Mosaic

OHIO STAR

For A, cut four beige/light-print 2½" squares and one rust 2½" square.

For B, cut two 3 3/16" squares of beige/light print and two 3 3/16" squares of rust print fabric. Cut each of these four squares on the diagonal twice, yielding eight triangles of each of the two colors.

Assemble the four units in the center of each side first, then sew these to the A squares as seen in the block picture, being careful to pin your seams so that you do not lose the points of the triangles as you sew. I press seams open when assembling triangles of this size, which aids in accuracy for piecing.

MOSAIC

Aunt Jo used a striped fabric for piece B, and if you do the same, be careful when cutting that you line up the stripes on each piece.

For A, cut two 4⅞" squares of beige/light print and cut them on the diagonal once, yielding four triangles.

For B, cut four rectangles 2" by 6" and then cut off two corners of each rectangle at a 45-degree angle to yield four parallelograms. Or, use the template provided (see pattern on page 180).

For C, cut one 3 5/16" square of the solid off-white fabric.

Make a template for the smallest circle as seen on the pattern page (see pattern on page 180) and cut five circles of the rust print fabric for the berries, remembering to leave at least ⅛" around the traced lines for turning under.

Stitch each A triangle to the long side of a B patch. Then, stitch each side of the C square to the shorter side of the B pieces, setting in the seams as you go around the square. Mark the ¼" seam allowance on the wrong side of each piece to maintain accuracy.

When you have finished piecing the block, appliqué the berries and embroider the stems.

Crosses and Losses

Evening Star

CROSSES AND LOSSES

For A, cut four 2½" squares of the beige/light print.

For B, cut five 2⅞" squares of the beige/light print and three 2⅞" squares of the rust print. Cut each of these squares once on the diagonal to yield ten beige/light triangles and six rust print triangles.

For C, cut one 4⅞" square of the rust print and cut it in once on the diagonal to yield two large triangles.

Sew a light triangle to each side of two of the small dark triangles. Sew each of these units to one of the two large rust triangles to form two square units.

Sew each of the remaining small light triangles to the remaining small dark triangles. Then, stitch these units to the light A pieces to form square units. Stitch these units to the units composed of triangles, using the block diagram as a reference.

EVENING STAR

For A, cut four 2½" beige/light-print squares.

For B, cut one 5³⁄₁₆" square of the beige/light print and cut it twice on the diagonal to yield four light triangles.

For C, cut four 2⅞" squares of the rust print. Cut each square once on the diagonal to yield eight dark triangles.

For D, cut one 4½" square of the rust print.

Make a template of cardboard or plastic and draw four hearts on light-blue print fabric. Cut ¼" outside the drawn line.

Assemble the C/B/C units first by sewing the long side of the dark C triangles to the short sides of the light B triangles.

Then, add A squares to each end of two C/B/C units. Sew a C/B/C unit to each of two opposite sides of D. Complete the assembly of the block as seen in the diagram.

Make a template for the large heart shape as seen on the pattern page that follows, and cut four hearts of the rust print fabric, remembering to leave at least ⅛" around the traced lines for turning under.

Appliqué four hearts in the center block.

Chimney Sweep

Log Cabin

CHIMNEY SWEEP

For A, cut two 2 3/16" squares of the beige/light print. Cut each square once on the diagonal to yield four triangles.

For B, cut two 3 7/8" squares of the beige/light print. Cut each square twice on the diagonal to yield eight beige/light-print triangles.

For C, cut eight 2 3/8" squares of the rust print, four 2 3/8" squares of the beige/light print, and one 2 3/8" square of the solid off-white fabric

The block is best pieced by sewing diagonal strips of patches and then joining the strips to finish. For example, start at the center of the block and stitch a light-print C on two opposite sides of the solid off-white C. Add a rust C to each end of the C/C/C unit. Then, sew the long side of triangle A to each end of the strip. This is the longest of the strips you will make for this block.

Inscribe the center patch as desired.

LOG CABIN (MAKE TWO)

Cut one 3½" square of the solid off-white fabric for the center of the block. This log cabin block has a larger center than usual to accommodate the appliqué.

Cut three leaves from a dark print for each block (see pattern on page 180).

Log cabin blocks are constructed by sewing strips around the center, starting at one side of the white block and continuing to add a strip to the next side, going around and around until the block is the desired size. Make it easy on yourself by just cutting out six or seven 1½" by 9" strips of light fabrics (perhaps including a couple of medium) and another six or seven strips of dark fabrics for each block. Keep the light values in one half and the darks on the other by sewing two light strips and then two dark strips until you hit about 9" square. (Note that Aunt Jo selected a medium value for the first of the light strips to create a frame around the appliqué in the center.) After stitching each strip, or log, trim the excess length. After all the blocks are quilted, trim them to the same size, which is about 8½" square. Auntie did not fuss with even strips, so do not sweat precision on this block. Appliqué the leaves in the center of each of the two blocks and embroider the stems.

Shoofly

SHOOFLY

For A, cut two 3½" squares of the solid off-white fabric and two 3½" squares of the green print. Cut each square diagonally once to yield four off-white triangles and four green triangles.

For B, cut four 3³⁄16" squares of the solid off-white fabric and one 3³⁄16" square of the green print.

Sew the long side of each off-white triangle to the long side of each green triangle. Arrange these square units with the B squares as shown in the photo. Assemble the block.

Make a template for the small heart shape (below), and cut one heart of the rust print fabric, remembering to leave at least ⅛" around the traced lines for turning under.

Appliqué the small heart in the center block.

RED HEXAGONS

Hexagon Wall Hanging, Pamela Weeks, Auburn, New Hampshire, 2018. Cotton, 45" by 32".

I documented two nineteenth-century quilts made by cutting hexagons of red fabric and placing smaller hexagons of batting and a multitude of prints on the larger red hexagon. The red hexagon edges are then turned under and sewn over the print, catching the batting, thus sewing, quilting, and binding each hexagonal block at the same time. A third quilt was made of pieced hexagons, and an off-white fabric was used as the backing and binding.

I love this little wall-hanging quilt because it contains many of my favorite fabrics from earlier projects, and it is a good one for taking along to appointments.

This wall hanging has 76 hexagons that measure 4½" tall by 5" across, and it measures 44" long by 31½" wide. I chose to arrange the hexagons for a narrow wall hanging, but you can arrange them as you please.

MATERIALS

- High-quality, 100% cottons fabrics are best for quilts.
- Large hexagons (in red): 2½ yards
- Smaller hexagons (in multiple scraps): total about 1¾ yards
- Batting: Purchase a crib-sized batting that is 45" by 60", or use scraps from previous projects.
- Cardboard or plastic template material
- Thread for hand or machine quilting

EQUIPMENT

- Rotary cutter, mat, and ruler
- Standard iron and small iron (optional)
- Straight pins
- Hand-quilting needles (if you choose to hand-quilt the center of each block)
- If desired, sewing machine with piecing foot and walking foot for quilting
- Scissors

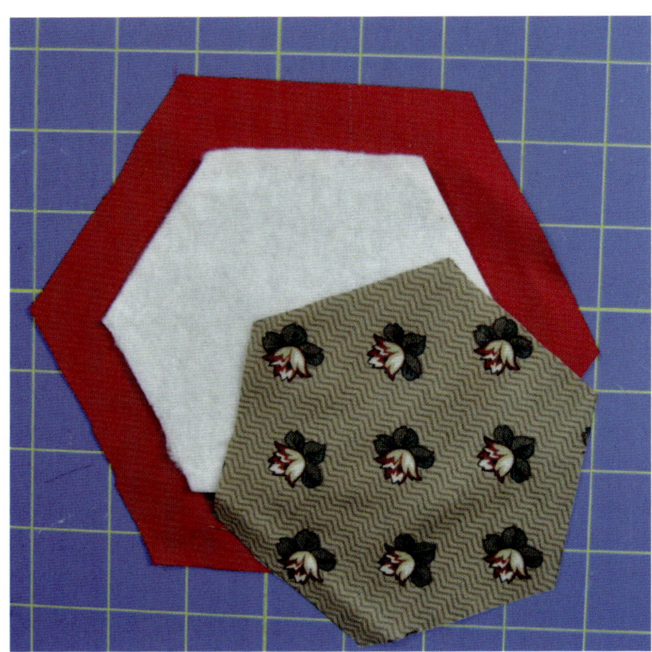

After cutting, prepare the layers for each block.

Prepare your fabrics for rotary cutting by pressing and layering them. I cut as many as six layers at a time. I also layered the many scraps used in this project and cut several at once. The same method worked for the batting, although I found I could cut only four layers at once.

Photocopy or trace the two hexagon patterns and create templates from plastic or cardboard.

With the larger hexagon pattern, cut 76 hexagons of the red or your background fabric.

With the smaller hexagon pattern, cut 76 hexagons of varied scraps and 76 hexagons of batting.

Place one red hexagon on your worktable. Center a smaller hexagon of batting on it. Then, place one smaller hexagon of printed fabric (right side up) on top of the batting. Pin the three layers together.

Turn the edges of the red hexagon up and over the

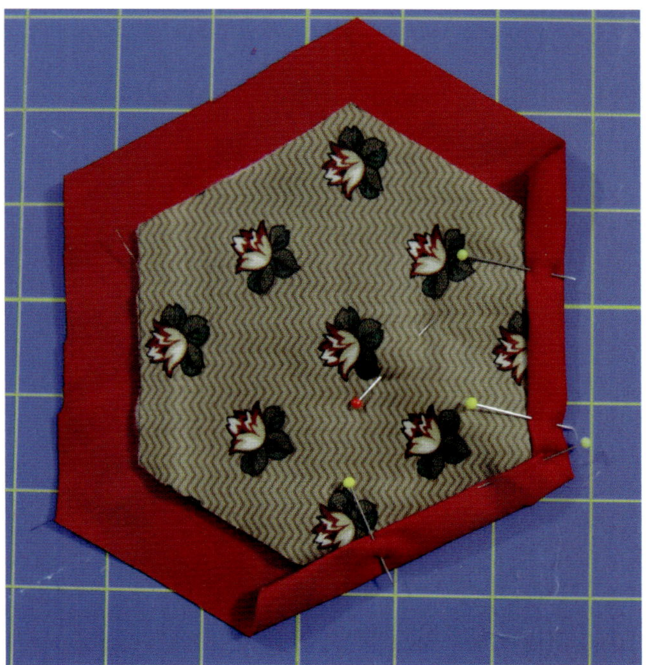

Turn under the edges twice, pin, and stitch, catching all the layers.

batting and print and turn the edges under. Pin in place.

If you want a completely portable project, hand-sew in place, taking a stitch through all layers. Or, after pinning, sew the edges with a sewing machine, which will catch all layers.

Once the units are complete, decide on the layout of your wall hanging. I chose to use varied-print scraps and sewed the blocks together as I made them. You may choose to carefully plan placement of your pieces. In either case, you will sew the blocks into a wall hanging by placing them right sides together and using an overcast stitch or whipstitch to secure each block to the block next to it.

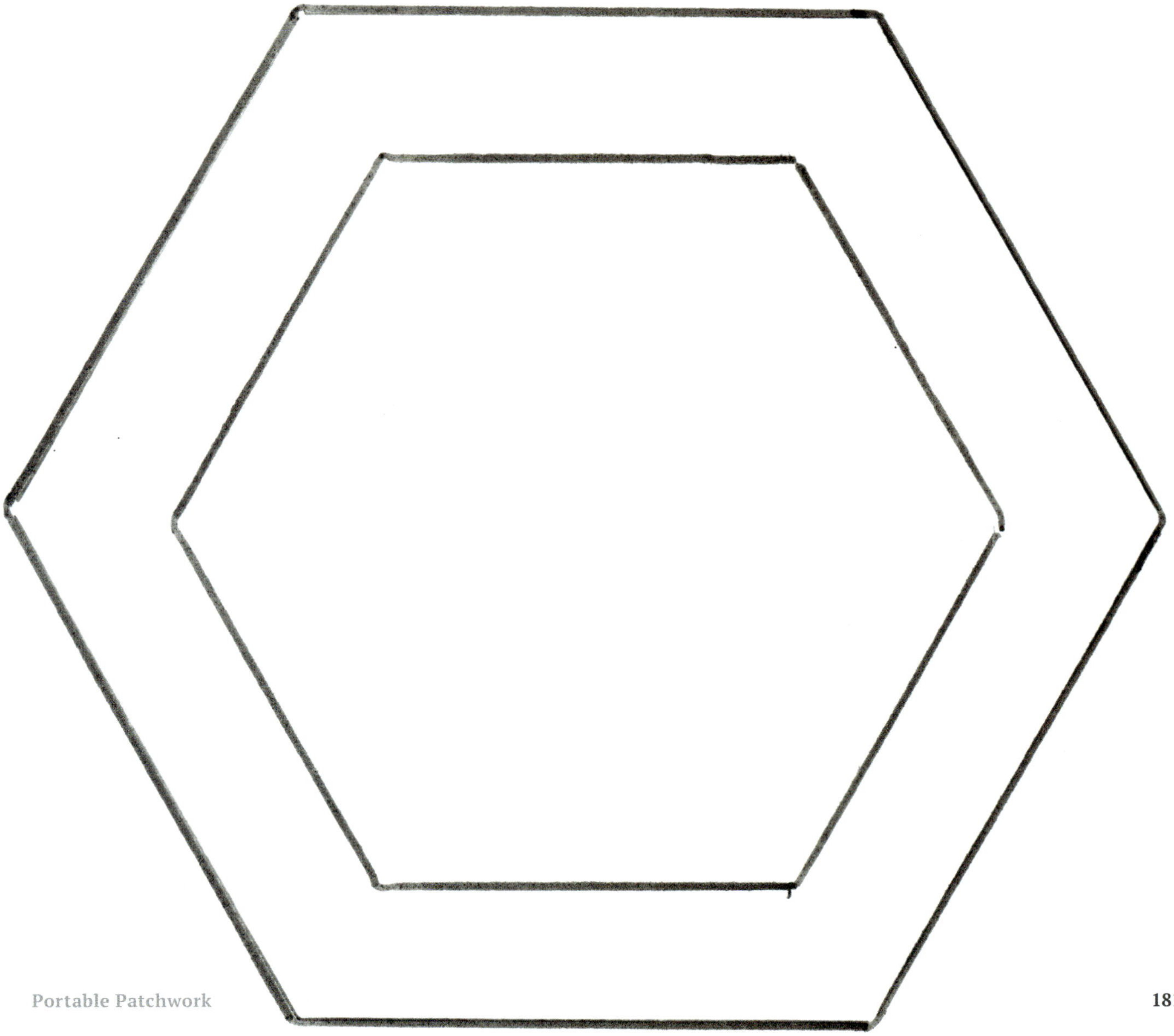

ADD A BLOCK QUILT

The Add a Block Quilt started with the author's collection of vintage embroidered samplers.

To make a fun and different wall hanging, individually bind and connect blocks of varying sizes and designs. Get used to the idea that there is no right or wrong way to do this project, since it involves making decisions about which blocks to include, which colors to use, and which different block sizes to use as you go along. You may end up with orphan finished blocks that you'll find other uses for.

The Ramsey Family quilt on page 148 is a great example of this fun way to make a quilt or wall hanging. The Ramsey quilt is made of motif blocks that have meaning to the maker and her family. Ramsey chose to leave spaces in the body of the work and left the edges uneven, which makes for a charming composition.

Another type of Add a Block quilt uses orphan blocks left from earlier projects, quilt blocks made or collected for the purpose, or a combination of both. I first made the Add a Block quilt that appears on page 158 to use a collection of circa 1930s butterfly blocks. I had such a project in mind when I began a collection of embroidered mottos and samplers, purchasing them in antiques shops and yard sales. I was charmed by the quaint and sometimes funny sayings they contained.

1. Gather your collection of blocks and, if they are vintage, check the pieces for stability and dirt. Wash the dirty

A variety of fabrics were auditioned for use in binding the blocks.

As the blocks were finished, the author played with their arrangement.

pieces in gentle soap and be sure to rinse thoroughly, but if you are using pieced blocks, be careful during washing not to shred the seam allowances. Press your blocks or pieces of embroidery from the back, and as you're looking them over, begin to think of binding colors for the blocks. For this grouping I chose to use harmonious blues, purples, pinks, and greens, with some red and yellow thrown in for fun. Many of the embroidered pieces were made in the 1970s, so to honor that, I used some vintage 1970s fabrics from my collection.

2. Determine your comfort level with "random." If you don't care about block sizes and will be happy with uneven edges and some empty spaces between blocks, skip to step 3. I prefer to leave no empty spaces, and so I work out a general plan for the proportions of the blocks.

I started by measuring the largest block, decided on an even number easily divisible by several others, and built that in for my first block. In this case, the largest block I intended to feature somewhere near the top and center of the composition needed to be cut down smaller than my desired finished block size of 12" × 24" due to soiling, so I made the decision to cut away the darker marks left from liberating the mounting sticky tape and added a border to the block. Then, I tried to make all the rest of the blocks some multiple of 2", 3", or 6".

As I built the quilt, I laid it out on the floor (or you can pin it to your design wall) and continued to add blocks, checking on the needed measurements as I added blocks. As seen in the photos, I arranged and then rearranged the blocks, added various sizes of sashing, or simply cut down the blocks and bound them to the size needed.

The Add a Block finished quilt

3. Build the quilt by laying out the finished blocks on the floor or on your design wall. Continue to add blocks, sewing them together in rows or sections. The best thing about using the potholder finishing method is that when it's done, it's done (except for sewing a sleeve on the back for hanging)!

Detail of the Churn Dash Potholder Quilt. *Photo by David Bohl*

EPILOGUE

While serving on the board of a locally managed nursing home, my paternal grandmother, Esther Marion Smith Weeks, helped dissolve the estates of incoming residents. After she made a donation, she brought home things that did not sell in their shop. She gave me two quilts in the early 1970s, years before I learned to appreciate antique textiles. I used and wore out the 1930s butterfly quilt, but the other one I never liked and never valued.

It was made in about 1890 and is a homely, red-and-white monkey wrench quilt. For many years it served as a Christmas tree skirt, and then it disappeared. A divorce and an impending move forced me up to the attic for one last look to make sure I had packed all my personal goods. I opened a trunk that was pushed far under the eaves, and there it was—my first potholder quilt, given to me by the grandmother who had so much influence on my life. She had unwittingly infected me with the potholder bug, but it had lain dormant for twenty-five years until the silk Sarah A. Leavitt quilt came to my collection and sparked the search for the origins of potholder quilts that resulted in this book.

Churn Dash Potholder Quilt, ca. 1890. Unknown maker, collected in New Hampshire. Cotton, 78" by 57". The beat-up little churn dash quilt was a gift to the author from her grandmother in the early 1970s, but it was hidden in a trunk for many years and not rediscovered until 2007. *Collection of the author; photo by David Bohl*

GLOSSARY

appliqué: From the French "to put on," appliqué is a technique used to create patterns by sewing or fusing pieces of fabric to a larger background fabric.

backing: The material used as the bottom layer or lining of a block or a quilt

basting: The method used to hold the sandwich of the block or quilt top, batting, and backing together while quilting the layers. Common techniques include using safety pins or long running stitches.

batting: The middle layer in a quilt or quilt block that provides warmth and texture and is sandwiched between the fabric in the top of the block and the lining or backing of the block

bias binding: Binding strips are cut at a 45-degree angle to the straight grain of the fabric, which makes it easier to bind a curve because it has more give than a strip cut on the straight grain.

binding: Strips of fabric sewn onto the edges of a block or quilt to encase and finish the raw edges

block: A repeated section of a quilt

borders: Plain or pieced strips of fabric that surround a quilt top, creating a frame

broderie-perse appliqué: From the French for "Persian embroidery," this is a style of appliqué that involves applying bits of fabric with printed designs—often flowers and other natural motifs—to create a new scene.

butted finish (*see* **knife-edge finish**): A method used to sew finished blocks together by placing them side by side and stitching them together invisibly. A second method is to place raw-edge blocks together, sew them with a zigzag stitch, and cover this seam with a narrow finished strip of fabric.

embroidery: The use of needle and thread to create images on fabric

filling: *See* batting.

fusible webbing: A material used to bond fabric or batting when heated with an iron

inscribed quilt: A quilt with written messages, signatures, dates, etc.

knife-edge finish: A method of finishing the edge of a block or the edge of a quilt that is achieved by folding the raw edges of the top and lining to the wrong side. These folded edges are lined up evenly, then sewn together invisibly to create a finished edge.

ladder stitch: A stitch used to invisibly make a seam or to join two finished units

lining: *See* backing.

piecing: The act of sewing together bits of cloth to make a design, usually geometric in character

potholder quilt: A quilt made of individually finished blocks or units of any shape or size

quilt: A textile made by sandwiching two pieces of fabric with batting and joining the layers with hand or machine stitching

quilt as you go (QAYG): A method of making a quilt in sections that are joined to make a larger quilt

raw edge: The unfinished edge of fabric, which tends to fray if left unfinished

repeating-block quilts: Quilts with tops made by making some or many blocks of the same pattern

sashing: The strips of fabric sewn between blocks; these strips may create another pattern on a quilt.

slip stitch: A concealed stitch for attaching two pieces of fabric by taking a small stitch in one fabric and then a small stitch in the adjacent fabric

straight-grain binding: Binding strips are cut lengthwise or across the grain of the fabric.

tile quilt: Also called stone wall quilts, tile quilts have randomly shaped pieces of fabric appliquéd to their surface, with a narrow bit of the background fabric showing around each piece—similar to the grout on a tile floor.

top: The part of the block or quilt that is intended to be most visible—its face

topstitching: Intentionally visible stitching on the top surface of a block or quilt

variety quilt: Quilt composed of blocks made in many different patterns. Variety quilts may include both pieced and appliqué designs.

wadding: *See* batting.

whipstitch: A visible, tightly overcast or overhand stitch resulting in a secure way to hold finished units together

woven tape: Also called cloth tape, woven tape is narrow woven fabric strips that may be used to finish the edges of blocks or quilts.

NOTES

CHAPTER 1

1. Bonnie Leman, *Quick and Easy Quilting* (Great Neck, NY: Hearthside, 1972).

CHAPTER 2

2. Louis Antoine Godey, ed., "Hexagon Patch-Work," *Godey's Lady's Book*, January 1835: 41.
3. S. Annie Frost, *The Ladies' Guide to Needle Work, Embroidery, etc.: Being a Complete Guide to All Kinds of Fancy Work* (New York: H. T. Williams, 1877), 128.
4. Wentzel quilt, Parkdale-Maplewood (Nova Scotia) Community Museum collection, accession number unknown.
5. Ruby Short McKim, *101 Patchwork Patterns* (New York: Dover, 1962), 79.
6. Robbie Fanning and Tony Fanning, *The Complete Book of Machine Quilting* (Radnor, PA: Chilton Book, 1980), 136, 213.
7. Janet Rae and Margaret Tucker, "Quilts with Special Associations," in *Quilt Treasures of Great Britain: The Heritage Search of the Quilters' Guild* (Nashville: Rutledge Hill, 1995), 181. The authors make distinctions among inscribed, autograph, and signature quilts. Loretta B. Chase, as cocurator of *Women's Writes*, an exhibit at the New England Quilt Museum, Lowell, Massachusetts, May–June 2010, suggests the more inclusive term "inscribed" in place of "signature."
8. Xenia Cord, "Signature Quilts, Part 1," on the website Celia Eddy's Quilt Story. The author discusses the differences between the public and private spheres of inscribed presentation quilts. Unfortunately, the website is no longer available.
9. Dorothy Cozart, "A Century of Fundraising Quilts, 1860–1960," in *Quiltmaking in America: Beyond the Myths*, ed. Laurel Hilton (Nashville: Rutledge Hill, 1994), 156–63.
10. Interview with Stephanie Hatch, July 30, 2006, at the Pine Tree Quilt Festival in Augusta, Maine.
11. Robert Bishop, William Secord, and Judith Reiter Weissman, *The Knopf Collectors' Guides to American Antiques: Quilts, Coverlets, Rugs and Samplers* (New York: Alfred A. Knopf, 1982), 21.
12. Washington County (MN) Historical Society collection, #1991.71.02; Brent Peterson, executive director, telephone interview, May 18, 2009.
13. New England Quilt Museum collection, #2000.02.

14. Historic New England collection, #1926.206.

15. Donald Beld, conversation with author, Boston, June 4, 2010. Beld collected and assembled potholder blocks for a variety quilt in May 2010 and then washed the quilt. Although the quilt softened considerably, several inscriptions were lost.

CHAPTER 3

16. Concord (MA) Museum collection, #T1822.

17. Concord (MA) Museum, accession file, #T1833.

18. John T. Hull, ed., *Centennial Celebration: An Account of the Municipal Celebration of the One Hundredth Anniversary of the Incorporation of the Town of Portland, July 4th, 5th, and 6th, 1886* (Portland, ME: Owen, Strout, 1886), 86.

19. John F. Bauman, *Gateway to Vacationland: The Making of Portland, Maine* (Amherst and Boston: University of Massachusetts Press, 2012), 24–26.

20. William Hutchinson Rowe, *The Maritime History of Maine: Three Centuries of Shipbuilding & Seafaring* (New York: W. W. Norton, 1948), 290–91.

21. Florence M. Montgomery, *Printed Textiles: English and American Cottons and Linens, 1700–1850* (New York: Viking, 1970), 338–39.

22. Ron Soodalter, *Hanging Captain Gordon: The Life and Trial of an American Slave Trader* (New York: Atria Books, 2006), 1.

23. Death Records from ancestry.com.

24. The research library of the New Hampshire Historical Society has in its collection six volumes by various authors on the Leavitt families originating in New Hampshire. The information for the selected Sarah A. Leavitt in this essay is from C. G. Steer, *Leavitts: The Leavitts of America; A Compilation of Five Branches & Gleanings from New England to California and Canada* (Salem, MA: Higginson Book, 1924).

25. Interview with June Hoyt, Manchester, New Hampshire, August 2002.

26. The Manchester Historical Association has a complete set of Manchester city directories in its collection, and I accessed the early ones several times for the information on the Leavitt, Noyes, Perry, Hill, and Hoyt families, including their occupations, businesses, and street addresses. The directories also list mills where the operators were employed. The early volumes include histories of the development of the cities and information on the various corporations such as capital invested, number of employees, number of looms, and annual output of yardage of fabrics.

27. Aurore Eaton, *The Amoskeag Manufacturing Company: A History of Enterprise on the Merrimack River* (Charleston, SC: History Press, 2015), 15.

28. Thomas Dublin, *Farm to Factory: Women's Letters, 1830–1860* (New York: Columbia University Press, 1993), 3.

29. Maurice D. Clarke, *Manchester: A Brief Record of Its Past and a Picture of Its Present, 1875* (Manchester, NH: John B. Clarke, 1875), 45.

30. Dublin, *Farm to Factory*, 7.

31. Godfrey Memorial Library, American Genealogical-Biographical Index (AGBI), accessed through Ancestry.com.

32. New Hampshire Probate Court (Hillsborough County), *New Hampshire, Wills and Probate Records, 1643–1982*, accessed through Ancestry.com.

33. The Hamlin Memorial Library and Museum website included a succinct history: www.hamlin.lib.me.us.

34. "Collar Made by Persis Sibley, ca. 1840," www.mainememory.net/artifact/16856.

35. Persis Sibley Andrews, diary (transcription), Hamlin Memorial Library, Paris Hill, Maine.

36. Ibid.

CHAPTER 4

37. Mrs. F. R. (Mary E.) Sweetser, *History of the Town of Cumberland Maine* (Yarmouth, ME: A. F. Tilton, 1921), 20–22, 33.

38. Sweetser, *History of the Town of Cumberland Maine*, 20–22.

39. One quilt may have been made as early as 1843. Its whereabouts are unknown, and the date may not be accurate.

40. The location of the Craig quilt is unknown. The LSC quilt sold at auction in 2010, before this research began, and is in private hands. The author was able to examine the quilt and photographed most of it before the sale. The Comet quilt is unavailable for examination, and its documentation remains incomplete.

41. Thomas C. Bennett, comp., *Vital Records of the Towns of Cumberland, Maine, 1983–1960* (Rockport, ME: Picton, 2005), 175–226.

42. Examination of the Fisherville Friendship quilt in April 2011. The quilt is in a private collection.

43. Valentine Richmond History Center collection, #V.80.160.

44. Registration form for the National Register of Historic Places, US Department of the Interior, National Park Service. April 21, 1993. Section 7, pages 1–5.

45. Ibid., 5.

46. 1850 United States Census records accessed on Ancestry.com.

47. Nancy Carlisle and Peter Harholdt, *Cherished Possessions: A New England Legacy* (Boston: Society for the Preservation of New England Antiquities, 2003), 166–67.

48. Examination of the quilt in May 2009.

49. Christopher Rhodes Elliot, *Howard Sunday School during Seventy-Five Years and the Work of Rev. S. H. Winkley* (Boston: Alfred Mudge & Son, 1902).

50. Probate of the will of Francis C. Manning, accessed through Ancestry.com. Suffolk County probate records, vol. 167 (1869).

51. National Museum of American History, object 1995.0011.04, gift of Mrs. Robert Stephens, https://americanhistory.si.edu/collections/search/object/nmah_556251.

52. Auction value website, accessed April 28, 2019. www.worthpoint.com/worthopedia/1853-historic-antique-poem-south-1864533720.

53. Sheila Buff, *Fire Engines in North America* (Secaucus, NJ: Wellfleet, 1991), 43.

54. L. Murray Young, *Iron Men and Iron Machines: Wakefield Fire Department, Wakefield, Mass.* (Magnolia, MA: Dick Weir, 1976), 12.

55. Ibid., 13.

56. From the opening page of the website What Is Freemasonry?, Grand Lodge of Ohio, www.freemason.com/how-to-join/what-is-freemasonry/.

57. David Greenland, *The Little Book of Freemasonry* (London: Green Umbrella, 2007), 62–69.

58. Email correspondence with Aimee Newell, PhD, then curator of collections, Scottish Rite Masonic Museum & Library, National Heritage Museum, March 9, 2011.

CHAPTER 5

59. Lynn A. Bonfield, "Quilts for Civil War Soldiers from Peacham, Vermont," in *Uncoverings 2001: Volume 22 of the Research papers of the American Quilt Study Group*, ed. Virginia Gunn (Lincoln, NE: American Quilt Study Group, 2001), 37–64.

60. Rev. Edward P. Smith, *Incidents of the United States Christian Commission* (Philadelphia: J. B. Lippincott, 1871).

61. Circular No. 10—Soldiers' Aid Society of Northern Ohio, Branch of United States Sanitary Commission, January 15, 1863, as quoted in Virginia Gunn, "Quilts for Union Soldiers in the Civil War," in *Uncoverings 1985: Volume 6 of*

the Research Papers of the American Quilt Study Group, ed. Sally Garoutte (Mill Valley, CA: American Quilt Study Group, 1986), 105.

62. Gunn, "Quilts for Union Soldiers," 114.
63. Mary Clark Brayton and Ellen F. Terry, *Our Acre and Its Harvest: Historical Sketch of the Soldiers' Aid Society of Northern Ohio* (Cleveland, OH: Fairbanks, Benedict, 1869), 62.
64. For more information on the inscriptions found on Civil War potholder quilts, see Virginia Eisemon, "Sunday School Scholars Quilt: Civil War Textile Document," in *Uncoverings 2004: Volume 25 of the Research Papers of the American Quilt Study Group*, ed. Kathlyn Sullivan (Lincoln, NE: American Quilt Study Group, 2004), 41–78; and Jennifer Regan, *American Quilts: A Sampler of Quilts and Their Stories* (New York: Gallery Books, 1989), 101–03.
65. Examination of the quilt at the James Julia Auction site in Fairfield, Maine, November 18, 2014, with Laurie LaBar. The quilt is now in the collection of the Maine State Museum, accession number 2105.11.1.
66. James Grant Wilson and John Fiske, eds., *Appleton's Cyclopedia of American Biography, Volume II* (New York: D. Appleton, 1887), 107.
67. There is an excellent and thoroughly researched Wikipedia entry on Neal Dow and his career in politics, the Union army, and his role as a national temperance leader. https://en.wikipedia.org/wiki/Neal_Dow.
68. J. Martin Skinner, ed., *Abstainers' Advocate* 9, no. 4 (April 1898): 62.
69. Research visit to the Yarmouth (ME) Historical Society, April 17, 2015.
70. *San Francisco City Directory for 1867*, accessed online August 10, 2019, https://archive.org/details/sanfranciscodire1867lang/page/n853.
71. Report of the State of California Department of Education for 1872, accessed on April 6, 2019, https://tinyurl.com/yxt6h5ko.
72. *Portland Sunday Telegram*, March 3, 1918.
73. The Yarmouth (ME) Historical Society has a scrapbook of undated and unreferenced newspaper clippings about the Prince sisters.

CHAPTER 6

74. 1867 nautical quilt, *Antiques Roadshow*, PBS, www.pbs.org/wgbh/roadshow/season/18/boise-id/appraisals/1867-nautical-quilt--201304A27.
75. Examination of the quilt, August 5, 2014.
76. The Maine federal naturalization records, accessed through Ancestry.com. Musaus swore allegiance on July 18, 1854, in Portland, Maine.
77. Birth, Death, and Marriage Records; Find A Grave Index; and Census Data from Ancestry.com. Also, Debra I. Grana and Marlene A. Groves, *Vital Records of Arrowsic, Maine, to the Year 1939* (Waterville, ME: Maine Genealogical Society, 2016).
78. Ibid.
79. Death Records from ancestry.com.
80. Marriage Records from ancestry.com.
81. Janet Rae, *The Quilts of the British Isles* (New York: E. P. Dutton, 1987), 107.
82. Donald F. Durnbaugh, ed., *Meet the Brethren* (Philadelphia: Brethren Press, 1984).
83. Interview with Gale Honeyman, October 26, 2009.
84. "J. A. Brubaker & Son," Miami County, Ohio, Genealogical Researchers, www.thetroyhistoricalsociety.org/Stories/Biograph/biog-ae/0020.htm.
85. *The Vindicator*, May 1942: 156.
86. I was given access to the documentation files of the Maine Quilt Heritage Project in 2008, where I found records of a number quilts made quilt as you go, including the hexagon quilts.
87. Eliza Jane Trimble Thompson, Mary McArthur Thompson Tuttle, Marie Thompson Rives, and Frances Elizabeth Willard, *Hillsboro Crusade Sketches and Family Records* (Cincinnati: Jennings & Graham, 1906), 143.
88. Frances E. Willard, *Woman and Temperance: Or, the Work and Workers of the Women's Christian Temperance Union* (Hartford, CT: Park, 1883), 77–78.
89. For more discussion on the Ohio Crusade quilt, see Ricky Clark, George W. Knepper, and Ellice Ronsheim, *Quilts in Community: Ohio's Traditions* (Nashville: Rutledge Hill, 1991), 149–52; Jacqueline Marx Atkins, *Shared Threads: Quilting Together—Past and Present* (New York: Viking Studio Books, 1994), 78; and Elaine Hedges, Pat Ferrero, and Julie Silber, *Hearts and Hands: Women, Quilts and American Society* (Nashville: Rutledge Hill, 1987), 85.
90. Tom Rademacher for the *Grand Rapids Press*, Grand Rapids, Michigan, October 30, 2011.
91. Inspection of the quilt, July 18, 2019.
92. The general historical information on the GAR was extracted from the website of the Sons of Union Civil War Soldiers, the organization that succeeded the GAR and still works to identify and preserve Civil War veterans' records. www.suvcw.org/?page_id=167.
93. Augusta Harvey Worthen, *The History of Sutton, New Hampshire* (Concord, NH: Republican Press Association, 1890), 518–20.
94. Adjutant Luther T. Townsend, *History of the Sixteenth Regiment, New Hampshire Volunteers* (Washington, DC: Norman T. Elliot, 1897), 354–55.
95. Author photographed the typed note during a visit to the Bradford Historical Society on June 15, 2009.

CHAPTER 7

96. The quilt was documented at the Madbury, New Hampshire, Town Hall along with the accompanying paperwork on November 17, 2008.
97. Richard Cleveland and Donna Bister, *Plain and Fancy: Vermont's People and Their Quilts as a Reflection of America* (Gualala, CA: Quilt Digest Press, 1991), 30–31.
98. The Town of Concord, Vermont, Municipal Plan, 2015. The plan contains a short history of the town and demographic information. www.concordvt.us/wp-content/uploads/2013/08/Concord-Town-Plan-adopted-7.7.15.pdf (accessed online August 29, 2019).
99. Interview with Laura Lane, June 19, 2019, at the New England Quilt Museum, Lowell, Massachusetts.
100. Access to United States census records via Ancestry.com.
101. Access to Clinton, Indiana, city directories via ancestry.com.
102. Naida Treadway Patterson, "Marion Cheever Whiteside Newton: Designer of Story Book Quilts, 1940–1965," in *Uncoverings 1995: Volume 16 of the Research Papers of the American Quilt Study Group*, ed. Virginia Gunn (San Francisco: American Quilt Study Group, 1995), 67–94.
103. Fanning and Fanning, *The Complete Book of Machine Quilting*, 136.

CHAPTER 8

104. Penny McMorris and Michael Kile, *The Art Quilt* (San Francisco: Quilt Digest Press, 1986), 24–29.
105. Eleanor Levie, *American Quiltmaking: 1970–2000* (Paducah, KY: American Quilter's Society, 2004), 14.
106. Robbie Fanning and Tony Fanning, *The Complete Book of Machine Quilting*, 2nd ed. (Radnor, PA: Chilton Book, 1994), ix.
107. Leman, *Quick and Easy Quilting*, 11.
108. Fanning and Fanning, *The Complete Book of Machine Quilting*, 1st ed., 136.
109. Marti Michell, *Machine Quilting in Sections* (Atlanta: Marti Michell, 2004), 5.
110. Telephone interview with Georgia Bonesteel in January 2019.
111. Telephone interview with Wendy Reed, September 18, 2019.
112 Ibid.
113. Personal correspondence with Cynthia Black, August 6, 2019.

BIBLIOGRAPHY

Atkins, Jacqueline Marx. *Shared Threads: Quilting Together—Past and Present.* New York: Viking Studio Books, 1994.

Bauman, John F. *Gateway to Vacationland: The Making of Portland, Maine.* Amherst and Boston: University of Massachusetts Press, 2012.

Baumgarten, Linda, and Kimberly Smith Ivey. *Four Centuries of Quilts.* New Haven, CT: Yale University Press, 2014.

Bennett, Thomas C., comp. *Vital Records of the Towns of Cumberland, Maine, 1893–1960.* Rockport, ME: Picton, 2005.

Bishop, Robert, William Secord, and Judith Reiter Weissman. *The Knopf Collectors' Guides to American Antiques: Quilts, Coverlets, Rugs and Samplers.* New York: Alfred A. Knopf, 1982.

Bonesteel, Georgia. *Lap Quilting with Georgia Bonesteel.* Birmingham, AL: Oxmoor House, 1982.

Bonfield, Lynn A. "Quilts for Civil War Soldiers from Peacham, Vermont." In *Uncoverings 2001: Volume 22 of the Research Papers of the American Quilt Study Group.* Edited by Virginia Gunn, 37–64. Lincoln, NE: American Quilt Study Group, 2001.

Botsford, Shirley. *Quilt-It-Yourself Log Cabin.* Simplicity #2076, 1994.

Brackman, Barbara. *Clues in the Calico: A Guide to Identifying and Dating Antique Quilts.* McLean, VA: EPM, 1989.

———. "Signature Quilts: Nineteenth-Century Trends." In *Quiltmaking in America: Beyond the Myths.* Edited by Laurel Horton, 23. Nashville: Rutledge Hill, 1994.

Brayton, Mary Clark, and Ellen F. Terry. *Our Acre and Its Harvest: Historical Sketch of the Soldiers' Aid Society of Northern Ohio.* Cleveland, OH: Fairbanks, Benedict, 1869.

Breckenridge, Muriel. *Lap Quilting: How to Make Beautiful Quilted Projects, Large and Small.* New York: Sterling, 1981.

Buff, Sheila. *Fire Engines in North America.* Secaucus, NJ: Wellfleet, 1991.

Carlisle, Nancy, and Peter Harholdt. *Cherished Possessions: A New England Legacy.* Boston: Society for the Preservation of New England Antiquities, 2003.

Clapp, Annis. *Made from Scratch Biscuit Quilts: 8 Rag Quilt Projects!* Little Rock, AR: Leisure Arts, 2004.

Clark, Ricky, George W. Knepper, and Ellice Ronsheim. *Quilts in Community: Ohio's Traditions.* Nashville: Rutledge Hill, 1991.

Clarke, Maurice D. *Manchester: A Brief Record of Its Past and a Picture of Its Present, 1875.* Manchester, NH: John B. Clarke, 1875.

Cleveland, Richard L., and Donna Bister. *Plain and Fancy: Vermont's People and Their Quilts as a Reflection of America.* Gualala, CA: Quilt Digest Press, 1991.

Clouston, Jennifer. *Foolproof Crazy Quilting.* Lafayette, CA: C&T, 2013.

Connecticut Quilt Search Project. *Quilts and Quiltmakers: Covering Connecticut.* Atglen, PA: Schiffer, 2002.

Cozart, Dorothy. "A Century of Fundraising Quilts, 1860–1960." In *Quiltmaking in America: Beyond the Myths.* Edited by Laurel Horton, 156–63. Nashville: Rutledge Hill, 1994.

Donahue, Nancy, and Cynthia Mullvain. *The Quilt as You Go Guide.* Chico, CA: Ink Spot, 1979.

Donaldson, Beth. *Block by Block: New Techniques for Machine Quilting and Assembly.* Bothell, WA: That Patchwork Place, 1995.

Dublin, Thomas. *Farm to Factory: Women's Letters, 1830–1860.* New York: Columbia University Press, 1993.

Durnbaugh, Donald F., ed. *Meet the Brethren.* Philadelphia: Brethren Press, 1984.

Eaton, Aurore. *The Amoskeag Manufacturing Company: A History of Enterprise on the Merrimack River.* Charleston, SC: History Press, 2015.

Eisemon, Virginia. "Sunday School Scholars Quilt: Civil War Textile Document." In *Uncoverings 2004: Volume 25 of the Research Papers of the American Quilt Study Group.* Edited by Kathlyn Sullivan, 41–78. Lincoln, NE: American Quilt Study Group, 2004.

Elliot, Christopher Rhodes. *Howard Sunday School during Seventy-Five Years and the Work of Rev. S. H. Winkley.* Boston: Alfred Mudge & Son, 1902. http://nrs.harvard.edu/urn-3:DIV.LIB:26553946 (accessed August 30, 2019).

Emmerson, Keryn. *Beautiful Quilts as You Go.* Paducah, KY: American Quilter's Society, 2005.

Fanning, Robbie, and Tony Fanning. *The Complete Book of Machine Quilting.* Radnor, PA: Chilton Book, 1980.

———. *The Complete Book of Machine Quilting.* 2nd ed. Radnor, PA: Chilton Book, 1994.

Fisher, Katharine, and Elizabeth Kay. *Quilting in Squares.* New York: Scribner & Sons, 1978.

Fons, Marianne, and Liz Porter. *Quilter's Complete Guide.* Little Rock, AR: Leisure Arts, 1993.

Forster, Carolyn. *Quilting-on-the-Go.* Lancing, UK: Teamwork Craftbooks, 2007.

Frager, Dorothy. *The Quilting Primer.* Radnor, PA: Chilton Book, 1974.

Freeman, Val. *Guide to Quilted Appliqué.* New York: Sterling, 1986.

Frost, S[arah] Annie. *The Ladies' Guide to Needle Work, Embroidery, etc.: Being a Complete Guide to All Kinds of Ladies' Fancy Work.* New York: H. T. Williams, 1877. https://catalog.hathitrust.org/Record/100166205.

Giesberg, Judith Ann. *Civil War Sisterhood: The US Sanitary Commission and Women's Politics in Transition.* Boston: Northeastern University Press, 2000.

Godey, Louis Antoine, ed. "Hexagon Patch-Work." *Godey's Lady's Book,* January 1835.

Gonsalves, Alyson Smith, ed. *Quilting and Patchwork.* Menlo Park, CA: Sunset Books, 1973.

Grana, Debra I., and Marlene A. Groves. *Vital Records of Arrowsic, Maine, to the Year 1939.* Waterville, ME: Maine Genealogical Society, 2016.

Greenland, David. *The Little Book of Freemasonry.* London: Green Umbrella, 2007.

Gunn, Virginia. "Quilts for Union Soldiers in the Civil War." In *Uncoverings 1985: Volume 6 of the Research Papers of the American Quilt Study Group.* Edited by Sally Garoutte, 95–121. Mill Valley, CA: American Quilt Study Group, 1986.

Hargrave, Harriet. *The Art of Classic Quiltmaking.* Lafayette, CA: C&T, 2000.

Heard, Audrey, and Beverly Pryor. *The Complete Guide to Quilting.* Des Moines, IA: Better Homes and Gardens, 1974.

Hedges, Elaine, Pat Ferrero, and Julie Silber. *Hearts and Hands: Women, Quilts and American Society.* Nashville: Rutledge Hill, 1987.

Hogan, Mary M. *Fast-Fold Hexies from Pre-cuts & Stash.* Urbandale, IA: Landauer, 2017.

Hull, John T., ed. *Centennial Celebration: An Account of the Municipal Celebration of the One Hundredth Anniversary of the Incorporation of the Town of Portland, July 4th, 5th, and 6th, 1886.* Portland, ME: Owen, Strout, 1886.

Kiracofe, Roderick, and Mary Elizabeth Johnson. *The American Quilt: A History of Cloth and Comfort, 1750–1950.* New York: Clarkson Potter, 1993.

Knox, Gerald, exec. ed. *Better Homes and Gardens Patchwork & Quilting.* Des Moines, IA: Meredith, 1977.

Laury, Jean Ray. *Quilts and Coverlets: A Contemporary Approach.* New York: Van Nostrand Reinhold, 1970.

Leman, Bonnie. *Quick and Easy Quilting.* Great Neck, NY: Hearthside, 1972.

Levie, Eleanor. *American Quiltmaking: 1970–2000.* Paducah, KY: American Quilter's Society, 2004.

McKim, Ruby Short. *101 Patchwork Patterns*. New York: Dover, 1962. Reprint of book first published in 1931.

McManus, Margureita, and Sarah Raffuse. *Crazy Shortcut Quilts: Quilt as You Go and Finish in Half the Time!* Iola, WI: Krause, 2007.

McMorris, Penny, and Michael Kile. *The Art Quilt*. San Francisco: Quilt Digest Press, 1986.

Michell, Marti. *Machine Quilting in Sections*. Atlanta: Marti Michell, 2004.

Millett, Sandra. *Quilt as You Go*. Radnor, PA: Chilton Book, 1982.

Montgomery, Florence M. *Printed Textiles: English and American Cottons and Linens, 1700–1850*. New York: Viking, 1970.

Murphy, Anita. *Reversible Quilts: An Easy New Technique*. San Marcos, CA: American School of Needlework, 1991.

Patterson, Naida Treadway. "Marion Cheever Whiteside Newton: Designer of Story Book Quilts, 1940–1965." In *Uncoverings 1995: Volume 16 of the Research Papers of the American Quilt Study Group*. Edited by Virginia Gunn, 67–94. San Francisco: American Quilt Study Group, 1995.

Pederson, Sharon. *Reversible Quilts, Two at a Time*. Woodinville, WA: Martingale, 2002.

Rae, Janet. *The Quilts of the British Isles*. New York: E. P. Dutton, 1987.

Rae, Janet, and Margaret Tucker. *Quilt Treasures of Great Britain: The Heritage Search of the Quilters' Guild*. Nashville: Rutledge Hill, 1995.

Regan, Jennifer. *American Quilts: A Sampler of Quilts and Their Stories*. New York: Gallery Books, 1989.

Risinger, Hettie. *Innovative Machine Quilting*. New York: Sterling, 1980.

Rowe, William Hutchinson. *The Maritime History of Maine: Three Centuries of Shipbuilding & Seafaring*. New York: W. W. Norton, 1948.

Sayer, Vivian L., and Anita B. Loscalzo. "Andersonville Prisoner of War Quilt." In *Massachusetts Quilts: Our Common Wealth*. Edited by Lynne Zacek Bassett, 252–56. Hanover, NH: University Press of New England, 2009.

Seward, Linda. *Successful Quilting: A Step-by-Step Guide to Mastering the Techniques of Piecing, Appliqué, and Quilting*. Emmaus, PA: Rodale, 1991.

Shaw, Madelyn, and Lynne Zacek Bassett. *Homefront and Battlefield: Quilts and Context in the Civil War*. Lowell, MA: American Textile History Museum, 2012.

Shaw, Robert. *American Quilts: The Democratic Art, 1780–2007*. New York: Sterling, 2009.

Skinner, J. Martin, ed. *Abstainers' Advocate* 9, no. 4 (April 1898).

Smith, Edward P., Rev. *Incidents of the United States Christian Commission*. Philadelphia: J. B. Lippincott, 1871.

Smith, Nancy, and Lynda Milligan. *Divide and Conquer! Quilt It Your Way*. Denver, CO: Possibilities, 2000.

Soodalter, Ron. *Hanging Captain Gordon: The Life and Trial of an American Slave Trader*. New York: Atria Books, 2006.

Steer, C. G. *Leavitts: The Leavitts of America; A Compilation of Five Branches & Gleanings from New England to California and Canada*. Salem, MA: Higginson Book, 1924.

Sweetser, Mrs. F. R. [Mary E.]. *History of the Town of Cumberland, Maine*. Yarmouth, ME: A. F. Tilton, 1921.

Thompson, Eliza Jane Trimble, Mary McArthur Thompson Tuttle, Marie Thompson Rives, and Frances Elizabeth Willard. *Hillsboro Crusade Sketches and Family Records*. Cincinnati: Jennings & Graham, 1906.

Townsend, Luther Tracy, Adjutant. *History of the Sixteenth Regiment, New Hampshire Volunteers*. Washington, DC: Norman T. Elliot, 1897.

Weeks, Pamela. "'One Foot Square, Quilted and Bound': A Study of Potholder Quilts." In *Uncoverings 2010: Volume 31 of the Research Papers of the American Quilt Study Group*. Edited by Laurel Horton, 131–60. Lincoln, NE: American Quilt Study Group, 2010.

Willard, Frances E. *Woman and Temperance: Or, the Work and Workers of the Woman's Christian Temperance Union*. Hartford, CT: Park, 1883.

Wilson, James Grant, and John Fiske, eds. *Appleton's Cyclopedia of American Biography, Volume II*. New York: D. Appleton, 1887.

Worthen, Augusta Harvey. *The History of Sutton, New Hampshire*. Concord, NH: Republican Press Association, 1890.

Young, L. Murray. *Iron Men and Iron Machines: Wakefield Fire Department, Wakefield, Mass*. Magnolia, MA: Dick Weir, 1976.

INDEX